Artists Observed

Artists Observed

Photographs by HARVEY STEIN

Preface by Cornell Capa

Essay by Elaine A. King

Harry N. Abrams, Inc., Publishers, New York

Contents

Frontispiece F. L. Schroder

George Segal

The creation of this book—a photographic tour de force—is the result of years of dedication. Its content embraces a good part of America's visual artistic community, a contemporary *Who's Who*, a veritable encyclopedia of creative artists whose works constitute the immense output and diversity of this country's culture.

Only a man of talent, imagination, and perception would attempt to capture in one insightful, fascinating photograph the likeness of a subject—as well as a characteristic fragment of his or her art and environment—and then multiply that feat more than one hundred times. Harvey Stein is that man.

Stein is a seasoned photographer with true empathy for his subjects, which is manifested by the human warmth this book radiates. He deserves our appreciation for his achievement.

Cornell Capa

Director
International Center of Photography

There is something intriguing about a portrait; it convinces through verisimilitude yet remains mysterious and limited. It can accurately resemble the person portrayed, but it does not convey complex information about the unique personality. How could it, when it represents only a moment in the life of the sitter? Portraits, however, can and do possess a powerful presence.

Throughout time the portrait has retained its importance in Western culture and continues to be an object of fascination. Before photography was invented in the nineteenth century, the human likeness was captured in various mediums. People have both a need and a desire to leave for future generations an essence of their being. The portrait can be seen as a type of testimony, a tangible trace of who we are and what we once were.

There is essentially nothing new about portraits. Although styles in portraiture have changed with the passing of time—angles of view, a sense of lighting, the choice of setting and artifacts within a portrait— ultimately what is left is a face in a context of some sort. Often that context and the artifacts depicted in the portrait are closely related to the social and economic life of the sitter.

Portraits can provide us with considerable information. They are not only a representation of the sitter, they also make a complex sociological statement about the era in which they were taken, providing us

Alex Katz

with data about class status, fashionable trends, and even sexual attitudes. Portraits can be viewed as the signature of a culture.

We continue to be intrigued with the never-ending pageant of faces representing each new generation because portraits deal with character. Within each portrait there exists a balance among fact, fiction, and structure, as well as reality and desire. Portraits enable us to see our commonality as human beings and our individuality. Portraits also document the procession of life from the cradle to the grave.

The photographic portrait is a young art form, existing only since 1839. As early as 1840, many miniaturist portrait painters turned to photography because there was a market for the new form. Rightly so, because photography was capable of yielding an accurate likeness more quickly and economically than painting and sculpture. Photography made portraiture available to a greater range of people in the nineteenth century, and it continues to provide millions of people around the world today with images and visual memories of important events and moments.

Within most portraits there exists a balance of idealization and abstraction. How that balance is realized is determined in part by the values of the age in which the portrait is made. In the works of William Henry Fox Talbot, David Octavius Hill and Robert Adamson, and Albert Sands Southworth and Josiah Johnson Hawes, we find unsurpassed examples of portraits taken with rudimentary equipment. This early portraiture is characterized by its formality of pose and setting. The long time exposures caused by the limited sensitivity of the photographic plates contributed to the lack of spontaneity in much early portraiture. However, despite the limitations the individuals cited above achieved remarkable results. The Victorians of the late nineteenth century were the creators of a "golden age" of studio portraiture. Julia Margaret Cameron and Lewis Carroll in England, Mathew Brady and Alexander Gardner in the United States, and Étienne Carjat and Nadar in France are among the finest of the photographers from this period. In the early years of the twentieth century, the pictorialists imbued their portraits with elements of artistic romanticism, with Peter Henry Emerson, Alvin Langdon Coburn, Gertrude Käsebier, Arnold Genthe, Alfred Stieglitz, and Edward Steichen representing a few among many. As the century progressed, an interest in realism and social awareness appeared both in Europe and the United States, and Jacob Riis, Lewis Hine, Paul Strand, and August Sander became leaders in this direction. Among the Farm Security Administration photographers of the 1930s, Walker Evans, Dorothea Lange, and Ben Shahn made outstanding portraits of working Americans, capturing their pain and plight during the depths of the Depression.

Portraits of the famous and the creative have always been popular. The genre has a rich history and comprises a large body of work. Photographers who have made exceptional portraits in this area include

Man Ray, Berenice Abbott, Gisèle Freund, Imogen Cunningham, Bill Brandt, and Brassaï. This tradition is exemplified today in the works of Irving Penn, Arnold Newman, and Richard Avedon.

Pictures of celebrated and creative individuals abound. There have been many museum exhibitions and books devoted to this category of portraiture, and we continue to be interested in discovering the person behind the creative act. Harvey Stein's current work is related to this genre and represents a fresh attempt to explore the realm of the creative.

In recent years many books have been written about creativity. Of all the efforts to obtain some understanding of the creative process, those recorded in Far Eastern anecdotes appear to me to be the most impressive. In the Chinese conception, the artist's ecstasy is a state in which the ego expands its boundaries, consciousness relinquishes its ties to reality, and the work being created is experienced as an extension of the artist's person. The creative experience is shared by the viewer of the completed work. An example of this state is described in the writings of Su Tung P'O (1035–1101): "When Wen Yu K'O painted bamboo, he perceived only bamboo in front of him and no people; not only did he not see people, but he lost all sensation of his own body, which also became bamboo. He thus became a new being."

Many of us want to know who artists are, what they look like, how and where they live, and in what conditions they conceive and execute their art. Per-haps, we may feel, a portrait of an artist represents a magical mirror that may reflect some added meaning about the artist's work and give us insights into the inner meaning of creativity itself. Harvey Stein's portraits of artists represent an exploration of the world of the creative.

Embarking on an investigative project such as this was not new for Harvey Stein. Having successfully completed a photographic study of twins, published as a book in 1978, Stein was familiar with the complications surrounding such a task. As with his project on twins, a sense of curiosity prompted him to begin exploring the world of visual artists in 1980. In this case, he not only made photographs, but conducted extensive interviews with each artist, aspiring to peek beneath the veneer of the external to see if something common was shared among creative personalities and other individuals.

The portraits presented in *Artists Observed* are a testimony not only to the photographer who produced this insightful body of work, but also to the artists depicted here. Creating a good portrait of any individual can be an extremely difficult task, and a good photographic portrait results from a curious collaboration, a transaction between the photographer and the sitter. When the right balance is struck, the resulting image can reveal something about the personalities of both the photographer and the subject photographed. Once the recording process begins, photographer and sitter become connected by a tenuous thread comprised of trust and awareness. A kind of ritual is enacted in the studio, and if the correct rapport has been established between the parties, the likelihood is high of creating a relevant portrait that reveals more than mere physical externals.

Stein's study provides the viewer with an opportunity to see a collection of many creators of our age in association with their art. The formal arrangement of each picture's setting works to enhance the portrayal of the artist's spirit and his work. This is particularly evident in the portraits of George Segal, Robert Rauschenberg, Lucas Samaras, and Alice Neel. Creating such a diverse and rich group of portraits is no small accomplishment.

Unlike some portrait photographers who resort to a method of formal stylization, each of Stein's portraits is a unique image, evoking the idiosyncratic nature of each artist in his or her environment. The success of each picture can be measured by the rapport achieved between the photographer and each of his subjects. The camera became Stein's key for unlocking doors into the realm of creativity, allowing him to explore, probe, and gain insights into the art-making world.

Stein deliberately chose to shoot these portraits in black and white. He felt that the sensuousness of color would interfere with the information and psychology he wanted to present: "I was interested in showing many aspects about the artist, and I wanted my viewer to concentrate on the artist and his art." Often color can become a distracting element, lessening the impact of the picture; black-and-white photographs compel us to concentrate on the presented forms within the picture plane.

Through Stein's impressive body of work we are witness to rare moments recorded on film. Presented here is a precise, complex, and poignant body of work. Collectively, these portraits represent a synthesis of art and psychology; yet each portrait is an individual piece, a reaction to a special moment. Perhaps Stein's study can only provide us with a peek into the realm of the creative; however, it is an important one. We are fortunate to have an opportunity to see the creators of our time; they and their symbols are reflections of our age.

Elaine A. King
Assistant Professor of Art History and Director, Carnegie-Mellon University Art Gallery

Ever since I was about ten years old, I wanted to create a book. I thought it would be the most meaningful thing I could ever do. It would be my way of saying, "I was here." It would be my stab at immortality.

As a teenager and young adult, I tried writing and painting, but with little success. Once I bought my first camera though—in 1964, while I was in the United States Army stationed in Germany—I knew I had found a medium through which I could express and communicate my concerns. Photography becomes more challenging and complex as I continue with it. Photography continues my education, for no matter at whom or what I point the camera, I focus on myself. Photography tells me what I'm interested in, helps to place me in this world, and provides me with new insights and perceptions. It involves me with living, being, seeing, doing, sharing, growing. For me, it is miraculous—still.

I love photography and I've always loved seeing art in museums, galleries, homes, art fairs, and public places. Frequently I have wondered about the people who made these marvelous objects and what motivated them. So why not combine my involvement in photography with my interest in art and artists? Indeed, why not? While completing several photography projects in the late 1970s, I casually began photographing a few artist friends. By 1980 I decided to more formally photograph and interview a number of artists to see what would result. I haven't stopped since.

My photographs and interviews present only a portion of the art world, but I believe it to be the most essential part—the creators themselves. Some of my intent for the book has been to investigate the myths that seem to prevail about artists: artists do little but live a very bohemian, rather free and crazy life; artists make art as an indulgence rather than as a serious, totally involved endeavor; artists are somehow, in their concerns and approaches to life, very different from the rest of us; artists don't need or care much about making an adequate living. I've found none of these beliefs to be even remotely true.

Another of my motivations for doing the book was to gain an understanding of what it is to be an artist in present-day America: to arrive at insights into the quality of the artist's life; to discover their sources of creativity; to learn how they survive and view success; to reveal their particular motivations, drives, and desires; to show how they relate to their art; and to explore some of the characteristics that seem necessary to being an artist. In short, I wanted to look at the artist from a somewhat sociological and psychological perspective.

Finally, I wanted to seek out and understand my own artistic roots and relevancies. In my desire to probe how and why others create, live, and function, I wanted to determine where, if at all, I fitted into that world. Whether I had to visit one or a thousand artists to accomplish all this mattered little to me.

Mary Frank

Presented here are eighty-five of the more than one hundred fifty artists I visited. I thank them all for their involvement, generosity, and patience. And especially, I apologize to those who, for various reasons, do not appear in this book.

In choosing artists to photograph and interview, I have made no attempt to be all-inclusive or to act as a curator. But I did seek out a diversity of art styles and modes, career levels, geographical locations, and reputations. The artists, mostly painters and sculptors, run the gamut from those who are very well known to some in mid-career, and to the emerging artists; the young painter just beginning a career has just as many illuminating things to say about that condition as the very famous artist has to reveal about a successful career.

My selections of artists were based on referrals, introductions, the availability and interest of the artists themselves, and occasionally, on my perception of how well their art would translate into the two-dimensional world of photography. But the focus always, for me, has been on the men and women who do the work, not on the art itself. Not everyone will agree with this approach, including some of the artists presented here; a few people declined to participate in my project on the grounds that the art, rather than the artist, should clearly speak for its creator.

The text that accompanies each photograph is taken from a tape-recorded interview I conducted with each artist. It has been edited for form and grammar but not content. The words are intended to expand the viewer's experience and knowledge of each artist and to explore more broadly the sense of being an artist. Mostly, the interviews centered on the state and the meaning of being an artist rather than on specific art works or the technical methods employed in the art-making process. Underlying themes that consistently emerged were the artist's involvement with his or her work; the need to create; idea generation and notions of creativity, inspiration, and discipline; the meaning of talent; ego; and the roles of fame and success. From these conversations, those elements that seemed to me the most illuminating, personal, and provocative were selected for presentation within the book's format.

In summary, I would like to offer these impressions concerning the artists and their work that I have garnered in six years of meeting with them:

—*The artists were uniformly intelligent and thought-provoking. Most were quite articulate about their work, were stimulating to photograph, talk to, and be with.*

—*Most artists seem quite egocentric. This is not to imply that they don't possess a world view, but rather that they are very aware of the necessity of creating out of the very stuff of their existences.*

—*Their work is totally important to them. It is the sphere around which their lives orbit. They are obsessed with their art making and think about it constantly, often to the exclusion of those around them.*

—*Talent is important for an artist to possess, but it is*

only the starting point. Many artists said that they know talented people who stopped working or who remain obscure due to poor working habits, self-abuse, or total indifference to their work from the art world. Discipline seems very necessary to the working process and is highly praised and coveted.

—Almost all artists maintain that suffering and poverty can only lead to difficulties in creating work rather than inspiring it. Hence, they completely debunk the myth of the starving artist.

—Artists claim that the most important aspect of success is recognition and respect from their peers rather than achieving a large public following or acquiring great wealth.

—Artists possess the same (if not more) anxieties, insecurities, ambitions, and feelings of competition as nonartists.

—Many artists feel united by the style or "school" of their art—abstract expressionism, realism, minimalism, etc.—and don't seem to have much to say to artists outside their group. This came as a surprise to me; I believed that since artists are all in "it" together, they would be more supportive and sympathetic to one another, regardless of the type of art they produced.

—Most artists work alone, but say they are good at it and are used to it. Some crave being alone and cite its importance to being an artist.

—Many artists feel they possess a God-given gift that must be shared with and communicated to the public. Some feel they are simply the medium or tool through which their art flows out to the world.

—Art critics are generally disliked; most artists claim they've never learned anything about their work from the critics, and some feel abused or neglected by them. Most dismiss critics as being irrelevant to their work.

—Most of those I photographed became artists because, as they claim, there were very few occupations that they could follow with as much conviction. Law, engineering, business, and medicine had little attraction. But it seemed almost by default that many became artists. As David Salle said to me, "I think it is something that I can do. You want to do what it is that you can do."

For the majority of artists, art making is everything; it gives meaning and shape to their lives and even seems to prolong them. Life without art would be inconceivable. And their lives breathe life into ours. I believe in their spirit, their hope and constant courage, their agony, their genius. To me, they are risk takers, innovators, and pioneers. They venture in a new world, sticking their noses and necks out where no one has gone before. So it is with the greatest amount of respect, awe, and love that I dedicate this book to them and to creative people everywhere. They deserve to be cherished. As long as I am able I will photograph the artist in America. It is too important to me to stop.

Harvey Stein
New York City

Index of Artists

Artists Observed

The man's the work.
Something doesn't come out of nothing.

Edward Hopper

An artist does not create what he sees, but what he is.

Anonymous

Raphael Soyer

Whenever I face a blank canvas, I feel some panic. There it is, absolutely white and blank, and I have to change it; it has to become something else. I have to deal, in my case, with a human figure and a background and a whole world on this very white canvas. I think the panic and its energy are a very good thing; they mean that I have no mechanical way of beginning and finishing a painting. Many artists start and finish a picture in a certain way; every canvas is the same thing. But to me every idea, every new painting, is a new thing. And there are always questions: "Will I be able to do what I want? Will I succeed with this idea?" Very often I do not succeed and I have to start all over again. That's OK; I'm satisfied with that. I always want it to be that way. I wouldn't like painting to become a habit, to begin and finish a certain way with every canvas the same. No, it should be always fresh, always as if I had never painted before.

I've painted for a very long time, but I don't get tired or bored by it; I love to do it. If I don't paint one day, I don't feel well physically or mentally. My eyes bother me when I don't paint. But when I paint a full day, I feel satisfied and everything seems to be OK. I would never stop, never retire. I can't see how people can retire; I don't understand that. My brother Moses died while he was painting. He was actually working on a painting, and the last words he said were to the model: "Phoebe, don't frown." Then he died. He worked to the very last minute.

Raphael Soyer, 1981

Kenneth Snelson

One of the fine critiques of my work that I've stored in my memory was from a show of large sculptures I had in New York's Bryant Park in 1968. Bryant Park is a place where people often come out from their offices on a nice day and eat their lunches. It isn't normally a place to go to see art. A friend of mine was doing a little film of the show, walking around the sculptures with a tape recorder and asking people sunbathing in the spring sunlight what they thought about the art. One man said, "What do I think of 'em? They're stupid, nothin' to 'em. They're like Bach or Beethoven." Now that's a statement an artist can appreciate. I wouldn't mind it as an epitaph.

Kenneth Snelson, 1980

Mattie Berhang, 1980

Mattie Berhang

My life experiences sharply influence my art. For instance, scuba diving gave me a feeling about objects suspended in a medium that I haven't sensed anywhere else. Scuba diving was one of the greatest experiences of my life. It gave me the sensation of being in a totally foreign situation. We all walk around in air constantly, but when you're in the water and weighted properly so there is no gravity, you have the sensation of being suspended in a medium, of being able to move your whole body with one finger because you are, in fact, weightless. This is a very foreign thing to our sensibility. It impressed me greatly, and the experience appeared in my work several years later. I haven't done any scuba diving since 1968, and I didn't begin making these mobiles until 1977. It took all that time for the diving experience to filter down, but the sensation was something I always tried to experience again. I think these mobiles are the closest I've gotten to it.

Philip Tsiaras

The general public has a mixed bag of opinions about artists. The man on the street thinks that an artist is someone different in society, could be an oddball, or might be somebody dressed funny. That's partly true but it's also incorrect. I think being an artist has gone up a rung on the hierarchical chain of professions and now has a certain glamour, given what Warhol and the whole public relations thing has done for artists. Artists are now experiencing a certain kind of renaissance. There are artists who are very rich, very successful socially; there are those with big studios and assistants galore doing a lot of their work; there are those with government sponsorship. Art has taken a swing to the right; it's abandoned the circle and fear of the leftist avant-garde. I think artists are very conservative in general; they are interested in all the things that constitute the American dream: fame, success, money, power, influence, opulence, penthouses, sex. Absolutely sex. I know many artists who want to make beautiful art in order to seduce beautiful people.

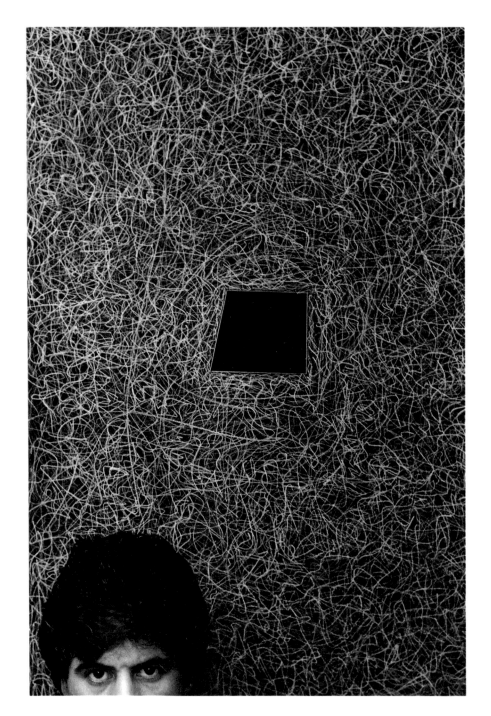

Philip Tsiaras, 1981

David Stoltz, 1981

David Stoltz

When I started out as an artist, the abstract expressionists were very important, and my art reflected that. But at a certain point I felt I couldn't go anywhere without representation. I reached a place where I felt I had gone as far as I could with steel in the abstract. Then these characters and objects started coming into my head. And I said, "Hey Stoltz, you're nuts. You make a star; who the hell makes a star. You're a thirty-eight-year-old man doing a star, little eggs, premortal little monsters; what are those things?" Who knows! What are they? I don't know. I do know that they are sculptural and three-dimensional forms. I like to think if I made one I could make a thousand or a hundred thousand. These characters just seem to rattle around in my head; they're sitting up there. They are wonderful little creatures, they're friends. I don't know who they are, I can't shake their hands, but they're friends. I think they have a life of their own, but that I'm very much in control of them. I hope I am. I never thought of them taking over my life. Sometimes when I go to sleep after working ten hours, instead of counting sheep I'll count little eggs jumping. Or maybe I'll dream about myself in these rooms with a million squiggles everywhere. It gets a bit obsessive; you can't help that. If one of them walked off and hit somebody in the head I'd be responsible and it would greatly affect my life. But I wouldn't like to think that one of my characters could do that.

Seeing this piece, I keep thinking I could have made it a little stronger, but one always has to feel that way. I have an idea for some figures that come right out of the wall, but that's for the next show. If I ever lose the sense of growth, I might as well stop being an artist and a human being. God knows, I don't want that to happen. You should be human first, an artist second. If I'm a human being first, the artist will follow. You can't do it the other way around; it would all fall apart.

Marisol

I never get stuck or bogged down on a piece because I trained myself that a mistake is not a mistake; so I don't make mistakes. Mistakes become part of my work and are OK. In school I was taught a philosophy of good and bad and that you always have to erase and do it again. I didn't want to have that problem; so I made up a kind of art that is either all a mistake or all not a mistake. I never erase or start over or redo something. I just leave it and work it through. I feel it's almost meant to be; it becomes part of the piece, and it never looks that bad because I'm not doing a kind of art that is so pure that if I chip it, there is a problem. If my work is a little bit dilapidated it looks better. I rarely ever destroy a piece or walk away from it—maybe once or twice. I feel very confident about my ability.

I like being well known; it doesn't get in the way of doing my art. Fame doesn't bother me because it's not as if I'm one of those people who made it overnight. I mean, if I am famous, I deserve it; there's a lot of thought behind my work. I feel that I am famous and that pleases me. It's a recognition of all the hard work I've done. It's not the kind of fame that some fashion model gets—there's a difference—that's just given to them. The recognition is important; it gives me a sense of security.

Marisol, 1981

Mary Beth McKenzie, 1980

Mary Beth McKenzie

I paint self-portraits as I see myself. Whether that is reality or not, it's my view. I don't try to reproduce reality exactly. I was hesitant about being photographed with my self-portrait because people usually look for an exact likeness, especially if I am in front of the painting, and that's not what a self-portrait is about. People will pick the painting apart on that level, going from the real person to the painted surface and saying that the two are not exactly alike. It's my view of myself, my reality, not necessarily an exact likeness. Everyone sees everyone differently anyway. A self-portrait is a composite of all the things I know about myself and all the experiences I've had.

I never want to paint just to keep on painting. I want to be taking a work somewhere. If I'm not sure where, then there's no point in continuing. I've discarded many paintings; it's a great feeling. If I am really stuck and having trouble and am terribly frustrated with a painting, there's nothing nicer than getting rid of it altogether. Usually I feel happy about letting it go; it's very freeing.

Maria Mijares

The important thing is that my paintings get done. They're within me and I'm doing them to share with civilization, not necessarily for the people who are alive today. I'm not sure how they will be seen. The important thing is to do the paintings, and ultimately I believe that they will be seen.

An artist operates on blind faith. You have to believe very strongly to want to continue to suffer and do the job. You have to really believe that what you are doing has value, regardless of your reputation, what everybody tells you, what the galleries believe, what art critics write, regardless of anything you get from the outside. Your art has to come from inside. Sure, I have self-doubts; I just spent three days trying to paint a two-inch rock and thought maybe I'd be better off wrapping produce in a supermarket. Everybody has difficult spots. Generally though, I feel that this is what I'm here to do. I never made a choice to be an artist. I am like a lamb; I am truly sacrificed to art because my life is not what is really important. Getting the paintings done is the only thing that matters.

Maria Mijares, 1980

Richard Estes

I do not pay too much attention to the fact that I'm called a photo-realist painter. It's only a category and is as good as anything else I could be called. If you're going to have any kind of success, you will be categorized somehow, good or bad. I don't think the impressionists liked being called impressionists. What does fauve mean, crazies or something like that? Nor did the cubists categorize themselves as cubists. The term was coined by outsiders. It's better to be called something than nothing.

I'm trying to maintain the tradition of painting in a classic, simple, intuitive way. I try to work in the tradition of Eakins, Degas, Vermeer, and the many other great realists. I'm an old-fashioned, academic painter trying to paint what I see. My format is pretty old-fashioned as well—just oil paint on canvas. The only modern aspect of my art is the subject matter; everything else is what has always been done in painting. Nor do I have any verbal theories behind the work; it's all looking at something and trying to paint it. I have never felt that the art of painting could serve any political or intellectual masters over itself.

Richard Estes, 1982

Larry Poons

There is no such thing as a well-established painter; that's the *New York Times* talking. History proves there is no such thing. You've just got to keep getting better; that's the only kind of hope that can exist for a working artist. That's the struggle: you've got to keep on getting better, no matter how so-called established you are. And making art doesn't have anything to do with whether the art is really good or not. You can always go on the assumption that it's not good enough yet, and you'd probably be right. The struggle is to not pay much attention to gross reactions, one way or the other. And certainly, it's not a question of being established. It's a question of continuing to make art and trying to make it better. That's it in a nutshell. I'm not going to mince words: one must try to make it better, always.

Larry Poons, 1982

Ilya Bolotowsky

I think, just as any average person can learn to speak, to walk, even to swim or ride a bicycle, anyone can develop a certain amount of artistic ability. It's innate. How important this is, is another question. I once met a young Eskimo soldier in Alaska. He wasn't brought up in our twentieth-century culture, so he makes a very good example. I asked him what he liked to draw. He laughed and said that he never drew. I asked why, and he answered that he had never had lessons. I said, "Don't talk to me about this; what are the other reasons?" He said, "I never had a pencil and paper," so I gave them to him and asked him to draw. He still claimed that he couldn't draw. I replied, "Why not? Every Eskimo can draw." This was a touch of racism in reverse. I meant that every man in a natural state can draw. So he asked me what he should draw, and I told him, "The various Eskimo occupations: fishing, hunting, building an igloo." He did it very easily and said, "I'm an Eskimo; I can draw." I said, "Of course, I knew it."

Ilya Bolotowsky, 1981

Tom Butter

I wouldn't want to be a painter because a painter is confronted with only a canvas and its surface. There aren't many choices in painting; one deals with a surface and a material. As a sculptor, I can do anything; I have a lot more choices. Painting has always been considered more intellectual than sculpture, but I don't believe that. In painting, there is a dialectic between the surface and the space; the paint is seemingly put behind the surface to create the feeling of space. Right away that involves a strange kind of intellectual tension. In sculpture the field can't be defined that easily. There are a lot of alternatives, from environmental to small ornaments.

Painting is limited, but the limits are clear. It's not limited in the sense that an artist can't do what he wants to do. There is such a variety of paintings; it's incredible, it's wonderful. I love painting, but I know painters who won't look at sculpture because it's too weird for them.

Tom Butter, 1981

Donald Lipski, 1983

Donald Lipski

Making my art is very serious play. People have said that it looks like I'm having fun; this is a concept I really don't identify with. I do have fun, I suppose, but it's more a sense of discovery than fun. The closest experience I can link it to is when I am in the library looking for something and it leads me to something else. I go from one book to another and one section of the library to another, and suddenly six hours have passed and I've been off in another world that I knew nothing about, but now I've learned so much that my mind is going in a thousand directions; I have a sense of discovery that's extraordinary.

When it's best for me here in the studio, I feel that sense of discovery. Occasionally I discover something that has the potential for changing my life, for changing my whole view of the world or some portion of it. How this happens in my work is so obscure, but my highest highs are then; it feels overwhelming. This is totally egocentric, but I would like to think that sometimes I make a discovery that can change the world. That idea is just a fantasy because I don't really believe that art affects the world at all except very tangentially, a tiny nudge perhaps. But at least it can affect other art, the art that follows it. There have been times in my life when I've made a piece I felt had that potential, and it's a wonderful feeling.

William King

Every time I see an artist who is really wacked out, I think, "There's another artist driven mad by the system." I was married to a very intelligent woman and a wonderful artist who said that the problem is not making the art but what happens to it after it's produced. Dealers, collectors, writers, all those people can drive you out of your gourd. I know a lot of artists who dropped liked flies. An artist may get a good start and then some jerk will write something unpleasant in the paper, and the artist will shrivel up. You deal with that by just keeping on and working.

I want my name in papers, always did. I want a good review. For one thing, if critics write about you, you eat. If they don't, you don't. If they write about you and say really scathing, vituperative things but it's a big review and there's a picture and they spell your name right, that's just as good as fulsome praise. That's because it's journalism, it's hype, advertising. If you get a big review, you are taken seriously. People think you must be important if a critic takes all that trouble to knock you. I love to get reviews. A bad review doesn't bother me anymore, as long as the work is reviewed, preferably with a big picture.

William King, 1982

Alex Katz

When I first started painting, I never thought I would sell my paintings. I thought that to pay the rent, I'd end up with a half-ass job at the Art Students League of New York, teaching or something. I was willing to paint at any expense: to live without heat for thirteen years, to not have children, to sacrifice any personal relationship—anything at all for the painting. I don't know why; I don't know what the heck drove me on to do it. I was a little simple-minded, I guess. I decided I was going to do it and do it flat out. At a certain point I knew I was going to keep going, but I wondered what the heck was going to happen. I think you can go on that way for a long time and end up kind of weird. You become a social fugitive. You get bitter living on the margin, on the fugitive side of society.

Alex Katz, 1983

Robert Ryman

Usually there are some people who see my paintings and say, "That's just white paint on a canvas; what is that? Is that art?" In fact someone came to my last show and asked, "Where are the paintings?" It takes a different awareness; you have to tune into the right frequency or you're not going to see anything. If you are used to seeing pictures in paintings and have never experienced painting in any other way, then you will look for something in the space of my paintings and will not see anything and will wonder what they are. It's just simply a matter of understanding what's there and being able to tune into it and, I hope, experience it— experience the light, the wonder, and maybe gain some enlightenment.

I'm not interested in white as a color; there's no meaning in white for me. The white is simply a neutral paint that can be used so that other aspects of the painting can be made clear: the surface, the texture, the edges, the color, light absorption and reflection, even the support that the paint is on. I am interested in slight nuances—the way the paint is put together and the way the whole structure of the painting is brought out by the neutral quality of the white. These qualities of painting are usually not even considered. Essentially, I use white as a means of opening up the visual aspects of the painting.

Robert Ryman, 1983

Ellsworth Kelly, 1984

Ellsworth Kelly

By removing the content (brush marks, subject matter, etc.) from my work I shifted the visual reality of painting to include the space around it.

The color, shape, and scale of my painting is not self-referential but relates to the walls, floor, ceiling, to everything outside itself.

Chuck Close

Boredom is an interesting issue. I'm not into boredom in the Warholian sense of the word; I don't get off on being bored. But I don't have the same feelings about working that I used to. I think one of the problems with our educational system is the notion that education should be fun; if we are having fun we must be on the right track. All those notions about being inspired, about having the muse touch you, about going into the studio always up and ready for a confrontation with the painting, and maintaining a high, intense level of battle with the painting are well and good; but this only generates certain kinds of art. I wouldn't want to be held captive by these notions of painting. We wouldn't ask a writer slumped over a typewriter six months into a novel whether he's having fun, because we have a different notion of what it's like to be a writer. Does he enjoy the activity of poking his fingers on a typewriter? No one asks a concert musician whether he's enjoyed all the hours of practice that enable him to walk on stage and perform. So I endure certain things that may seem boring or tedious; it's a trade-off I am perfectly willing to make because I produce something I consider valuable.

I have a professional commitment to painting and I do what's necessary to make art. There are times when I am bored doing my work, but it's not boredom in the normal sense: to sustain the same attitude long enough to pull off a piece that takes months and months to do gets tiresome, which means that I can't worry about how I feel when I paint. I have to go into the studio and paint whether I feel like it or not.

Chuck Close, 1981

Rodney Ripps, 1981

Rodney Ripps

If you are a fool you may not want to make money. The whole notion of struggling and being poor to do art is a myth. I have desires in my life other than my art. My wife and traveling, for instance, are a large part of my life outside of being an artist. I think the people who are happiest do the best work, and the best art is positive art, whether it's visual art or music. I don't believe Mozart was depressed when he wrote his music. I feel good when I hear it.

Who you are as an artist rubs off on your work; I would always prefer to do art that welcomes life rather than resists it. And I think living well or living the way you wish breeds the best art. Being poor inhibits the making of art. It's simply not true that success makes artists less hungry and creative; I work harder now than I've ever worked in my life. I'm very grateful for whatever success I've achieved and just try to turn that feeling into stronger work.

Jonathan Borofsky

I've been interviewed and photographed a lot in the past couple of years; so I've had my share of publicity. Each time, I feel a certain commitment to a public to be interviewed and to lay myself open and have people know me. But a certain amount of privacy is lost; right now I feel I need to pull back for a while. I am now being interviewed and photographed, and it will be printed in some book and can be read by a lot of people who don't know me. This can make me feel too self-important or throw the focus on the wrong things. The spotlight shouldn't be on me. The work is important, not me particularly or my life or my success or failure. It's not important to make a media star out of me, which is what book publishers or magazine people have to do to sell their products. Artists become the units that have to be made to look good so these products can be sold.

Sure, the person behind the art is important. There's nothing wrong with an interview. I'm saying that I've had so many of them, that I'd just as soon wait to do an important one—maybe in ten years or two years or so. I get requests every day from people to do something, and it's just a question of losing my freedom. There was a period when nobody asked me for anything; now it's the other extreme, and they are both not too pleasant. I'd rather have something in-between.

Jonathan Borofsky, 1982

Robert Birmelin

A lot of things in my paintings are based on direct observation; other things I invent. When I paint these pictures I invent the street, even though it would be possible to go outside and work from direct observation. I have to make myself believe that the street can contain figures in action. I work rapidly with acrylics, keeping the painting in a very sketchy, loose state for a long time. I may take a figure on the right side of the canvas and relocate it three or four times before it winds up on the left edge; the figure may change age, sex, costume, and function in the course of its journey. Somehow I need to experience those figures moving through the picture space. Such a process of constantly repainting may seem wasteful, but the movement has to be kept going long enough for me to feel its potential for becoming real. It's almost as if a crowd has to literally walk through the damn painting and shift around before I can start to lock any parts in place; even once their positions are more or less set, the sex, race, gesture, and expression are all very much up for grabs until the last strokes on the painting. A live painting is always open to this kind of change. It is an odd procedure. Sometimes I think of all those other figures buried under the final, covering layer of paint.

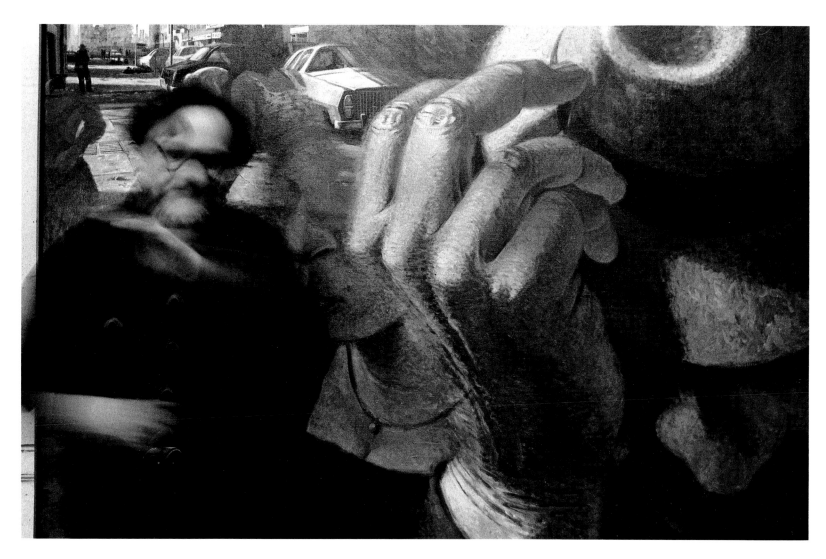

Robert Birmelin, 1984

Ed Moses, 1983

Ed Moses

In those periods when I'm not actually painting, I'm thinking about it and I'm not thinking about it, and I'm generally not pleased with the situation. I'm just sort of knocking around. I'll sit here and read, or I'll walk down to the beach and then call somebody up. I'll sleep for a while, go into town, go to a movie. Then something starts to happen and I'll get back to painting, but I'll feel a tremendous resistance, and the resistance becomes like a pressure cooker. Finally it pops out, a seam breaks, and then I'm cooking, so to speak. Then I'm paying my way. The rest of the time I'm just screwing around.

When I get something cooking, I run out immediately—go to the beach, to a bar, a local place to hang out and bullshit around. In about two hours I'll run back to the studio, turn the lights on, and look in the room again. It's like something's alive, cooking in there, and it's weird. I'll say, "Wow, you're too much," and then I shut off the light and run out again. The next day I start painting again, and once I get into it, I can work all day, around the clock. But I won't be a recluse; I still go out, still do the same shit as I did before. I'll work for two or three hours, and because I have to wait for the paint to set, I'll go out, maybe in the evening for three or four hours, and then I'll come back and make another pass. I'll work for another few hours, go to sleep, maybe wake up at three or four in the morning and do more, sleep again, wake up about nine, work on it again, and then go out to breakfast. Then I'll come back, paint, go out to lunch about two or three o'clock with a friend, and come back to paint until dinner. Out again, back again; so I just go around like that. It seems such a rush, a whirl, but things are happening. When I really get into it, I don't go out at all. Someone will bring food to me and I'll sit in that chair. Rather than get in bed and sleep, I just sit in that chair. I'll sleep for a half hour, then work for a couple of hours, and on and on until it ends.

Someday, of course, the pressure cooker might not pop. That's always the terror. It's horrible to be in those dry periods. The terror is also that this activity is your last link with the human species and with life. After that, what do you do? You sit around somewhere and disappear.

F. L. Schroder

I think the whole philosophy of New York City, its speed and turbulence, affects me psychically and affects my work in terms of its movement, color relationships, and segmentation. The energy that evolves in the community—in terms of music, visual arts, and theater—has a strong physical relationship to my work. It inherently affects a lot of decisions I make about my activity as a painter and a sculptor. New York provides space, impact, feedback, and intensity. If I were in Chicago or Denver or Kansas City, I'm sure my work would be different because the environment and its activity affect a whole stream of connections—the electricity, the current of things. Just being able to exist in New York plays a vital role in my effort to make art. There's a certain kind of communication in the environment that makes it important to be here. The frequency and current are definitely happening in New York. It's still the most important planet to be in.

F. L. Schroder, 1982

Hannah Wilke, 1980

Hannah Wilke

My mother understands why I've used myself nude in some of my artworks, possibly because she lived, when she was young, in an age where women were conditioned to be ashamed of themselves. As an adult, her introversion kept her safe. But I think she recognizes that the safety might have hurt her emotionally, even giving her illness and disease. And having been subjugated by that kind of pressure from society, I think she's very proud of my thwarting that which has been taught by culture but which I think is inhumane. She's always backed me and I'm very proud to be her daughter. I think most of my work really is for her. Recently I saw some funny photographs of her when she was about sixteen. She was really beautiful then, much prettier than I will ever be. You could see that little glimmer in her eye at sixteen. She was carrying on and looking good and flirting. People like to carry on, but they are ashamed of it. It's very sad. Why don't we allow children to draw on the walls and pee on the floor and be bad? We call it bad, and yet it's expressing their joy of living. And here we have to be adults all the time; I think it causes us a lot of pain. The idea of taking that chance to be stupid or to laugh too loudly or to be vulgar is, I think, the only way to create a work of art.

It's hard making art. It's boring sometimes; it hurts my eyes. I can't figure out whether my finger is stiff from arthritis or from drawing. Possibly I'm drawing with a nervousness in my pinkie. It might just be from drawing, but it is hurting me. That delicate drawing takes so much energy. To be calm and cool and collected, to be able to sit down and do those drawings, I almost have to wipe out my mind. I have to lose my mind to be able to concentrate.

Judy Levy, 1980

Judy Levy

I have a strong need to paint; if I don't paint I cry and get bad headaches. I once went six months without painting; I was putting my creative energy into designing hats. If I don't paint now I'm really bad news and depression sets in. I try to paint every day but sometimes I can't. I've got to paint at least a few days a week not to get crazy.

For me, there's a certain mood in which I paint best: a violent mood. When I become anxious and tense, a strong power results. Then I paint very fast, and I feel a release of pressure somewhere in my head. If I don't paint, maybe I'll tap-dance to relieve the pressure.

Painting is something I must do. It's an energy that just flows out of me. It's emotional. Sometimes I cry before I paint. I don't know why; it just happens. I cry, and then I say to myself that I'd better paint; the energy is ready to come out. I cry a lot, for different reasons, when I'm not too happy. When I'm happy, I never paint.

There's a sense of power to painting. I always feel great after I've painted—totally elated. I feel complete. It's like an orgasm. It's better than sex. It is. After you have sex you feel kind of empty, but after you paint you feel full. Art or sex, which one is it? It's a hard choice. It depends on how horny I am. Besides, if I have too much sex I can't paint well.

I think openings are bullshit. Everyone's just trying to get laid. I've been propositioned a lot: "I'll give you a show if you sleep with me." It happens often. Would I do it for a show? Now I would, but when I was younger I wouldn't. I wouldn't because I was a jerk.

Martha Clark

What I discover while I'm painting is all-important to me. Some artists have an idea and a picture in their mind of what they want, and they can execute that, but I'll start with an idea and often end up with something entirely different. I might make a mistake while painting that will take me in another direction, and I'll use that direction instead of what I originally intended. The painting then starts to become its own self. I'm sort of moving the pieces, but the painting is also coming out of the canvas by itself. But I must be able to detect this; that's part of what an artist does. This doesn't mean that I'm not in control of the work; I'm always in control of it. I don't believe a power out there is guiding my hand, no. I'm just taking advantage of the process; it's the way I work. As I go along, the painting changes, and I have to change with it or else the painting will fail. I'm leading it and following it at the same time. It sounds as though the painting were outside me, but it's not; it's inside me. It's both, probably.

It can be very exciting when I suddenly realize that I'm seeing a new possibility. To me, that's what the creative process is about. It's always being open to discovery and not doing something you already know.

Martha Clark, 1983

Robert Hudson

For me, the thought process in painting is harder than in sculpture. I think sculpture is easier because it is altered when the viewer moves even an inch or two; so it's more open to possibilities. I switched from painting back to making sculptures because I found myself spending months on one painting, and it got to be a drag. I kept trying to get too much onto the canvas; I think I was getting bogged down.

Although I can spend months on a sculpture, I will start several others during that time. I usually build ten or twelve sculptures and then paint them. I then have the fun of painting, but I don't have to figure out as much as I would with a canvas. In painting the sculptures, I can create illusions and get color onto something that's already there. The sculptures exist one way, but then I paint them and they become something else. I love that effect. Painting the sculptures expands them.

Robert Hudson, 1984

Barbara Schwartz

I find I'm now far more clear about my sources—things that inspire me, things I'm actually working from—than I ever was. I don't think, except for maybe a few early pieces, that I've ever done anything that doesn't have what I would consider very specific, source-oriented content. Whether it happens to be a leaf or a shell or a sailboat, it's always some interpretation of a real form or a real phenomenon. Most of my sources are from nature. I go walking through the countryside or along the beach at every opportunity. I was invited to work at Artpark during the summer of 1976, and there I worked with large boulders. That work was a terrific crystallization of how my sources originated. It was at Artpark that I worked three-dimensionally for the first time, opening up many new possibilities and directions. And traveling to Bali in 1979/80, I found images in the landscape and aspects of the culture that continue to influence my work and my thinking today.

I look forward to the time when there will be other environments in which to work because I believe you strongly reflect where you are. Every time I change studios, my work changes. The fact that my studio is in a basement right now—I don't have any natural light except for a small skylight—makes me more driven to do colorful work concerned with light and space. It's almost as if I'm working in opposition to where I am. In New York City I find I want to make things about nature.

Barbara Schwartz, 1982

Philip Pearlstein

Each year I've completed more work, partly because of the pressure to produce and partly because I feel more sure of myself. After a certain point you can't knock work out and still have it taken seriously. Each work has to be done as intensely as possible. The pressure on me is not a problem, but an opportunity to do what I've always wanted to do most—to make more pictures. And I want to do more, even though I've done so many, because it's what I do. Making pictures is my work. Some artists have the good grace of getting sick or killed young, so there is a smaller body of their work. Why did Picasso go on and on and on? It's a drive.

I don't see why painting should get easier. Someone once said that, in a sense, an artist needs a problem he can't solve. The lucky ones get into a problem that is unsolvable, so they keep going and there's growth, evolution. What I'm doing I'll never be able to really do completely. I know what I want to do: compositional schemes allied with closely observed reality. I try to paint what I see but I can't fully do it, and that's good because I keep trying to get as close as possible.

Philip Pearlstein, 1981

Al Held

Problems to an artist are life. They turn me on and are always changing. Five years ago my problems were somewhat different. They aren't radically different problems today but are different enough to keep the blood flowing. The problems keep me frustrated in terms of content, in terms of how to do certain things, even should I do them. Some people have said that all problems in an artist's studio are to keep the blood flowing and are otherwise irrelevant. I don't agree, but I can see that problems are useful for keeping things interesting and inhibiting boredom and static repeats. I have problems with technique; the technique keeps changing because the ideas change, and that's interesting to me.

I don't believe I solve problems; I think they are replaced with other problems that become more challenging. I might be working on a problem and then something else happens; I say, "That's curious," and soon the so-called prime problem gets put into a secondary role because another problem that's introduced seems more relevant. Problems are like some relationships; they just fade away. I don't necessarily give up on them or solve them; they either wander off or are put on a back shelf. Some calm down and become less interesting. If I solved them, I would paint the ultimate painting and I don't think there is such a thing. Certain artists, Ad Reinhardt for instance, thought the ultimate painting was possible. I don't. I think of painting as a language, and there can't be an ultimate language. Painting is an ongoing and evolutionary process.

Al Held, 1983

Tony Delap

One of the necessary qualities of being an artist, when starting out at least, is to not expect an awful lot, to be somewhat dense about any thoughts of what you will get out of being an artist. The artists I've known who have done important things are people who started out not even knowing why they were doing art. They obviously had the inspiration to take a crack at it, but they weren't asking for a lot. As a teacher I now see many young people who want to be artists but who appear to be quite desperate about what they'll get out of it before they've really begun. They're concerned about fame, fortune, attention, financial rewards. I think it's best to have the craze to be an artist but not to be too cunning and calculating about what the outcome will be.

Tony Delap, 1985

Kenneth Noland

It takes me three or four or five years to make changes in my work. I suffer just as much anxiety and have just as much feeling of being lost as I did as a younger man, when I also had to go through these work changes. I have to work my way through, and it takes years until I can get to a point again where all of that messing around and difficulty comes to fruition, into a clear, new phase of work. And that phase might only last six months.

Right now I'm painting easily and the paintings are clear to me. I'll continue as long as the pictures keep suggesting and evolving into themes and variations. But the minute the paintings start to get automatic, I'll have to go on and find something else. I find something else by playing around. It's like a baby playing around; it hurts not knowing what you are going to do and what's going to happen. It's a scary time. The messing around can last four or five years and result in awkward things. And it becomes part of the character of the paintings. Between each fruitful phase are long periods of exploration, faltering, learning, and working out things. And it all affects the criticism of your work, the sales of your work, your moods, and the way you live. It makes you harder to be around.

Kenneth Noland, 1982

Walter Steding

I paint personalities because with personalities, I can get the message across quicker, the message of portrait painter, 1982. Painting an ordinary person doesn't carry as much weight because portraiture is normally associated with paintings of famous people. Historically, only those who could afford it had their portraits painted. Now it's become a symbol, a norm, to have famous people in paintings. And it adds interest to recognize someone in a painting. It doesn't particularly add interest to me as the painter because a lot of interesting faces aren't famous. But I can put some funny white hair and sunken cheeks on a face and right away everyone knows it's Andy Warhol.

I always wanted to paint William Burroughs; I actually was introduced to him through some friends. I asked if I could paint him, and just like that he said yes. He was really cooperative; he sat for me and got out all his weapons and knives and tried to find the right look. It took one sitting to do sketches and a bunch of Polaroids; then I finished the painting in my studio. Since I was under pressure to do it for an exhibition, it took me only two weeks to complete; it all went pretty quickly.

Walter Steding, 1982

Robert Longo, 1982

Robert Longo

I don't view the artist as a person who sits in the studio and waits for images to appear in his head. I think the artist has to be a guardian of the culture. We live in such a highly refined visual world that what we know can't be ignored. In that sense, I take images from the world, redefine them, and give them back to the world. I'm here making sure the bureaucrats are not going to slip anything over on us through television and other media. I'm real interested in the seductive quality of the visual mode, particularly in American culture; it's so refined it's unbelievable. Our eyes and our visual vocabulary are just monstrous at this point.

A few other artists and I are the people who have preceded the Betamax. We are reediting and reorganizing the culture so that people can really look at what they're looking at. My work has a very violent edge to it, but it also has beauty. All these contradictions are very important in understanding the world we live in. Ultimately, art can provide two things: inspiration and influence. But artists have a chronic problem, a Cassandra curse: they can see the future but they can't really change it.

Carole Jeane Feuerman, 1982

Carole Jeane Feuerman

I think if I weren't an artist, I would be dead. To me, being an artist is life. I could stop doing art for a while; I once stopped for almost two years, when I didn't do very much, but my mind never stopped.

Once I woke up and my right hand was paralyzed. Being right-handed, a sculptor, and an artist, I couldn't tell you what my right hand being paralyzed would mean. Every time I moved my hand I was in excruciating pain. I never knew what it was; it disappeared, thank God, as mysteriously as it came. It lasted about two weeks, and while it was occurring I thought a lot about what I would do if I didn't have the use of the hand. I decided that it wouldn't really get in the way of my art. It would temporarily, but not in the long run because anything that I'm going to create has to come from my mind, not from my hand; so I shouldn't get hung up on the hand thing. If my work is really going to be good, it will come from within me and I'll figure out how to do it. If I should have to work with my other hand, so be it. I'd figure out a way. I have a habit here; I really am a junkie to my art.

Robert Arneson

The use of words is important in my work because it provides another way of seeing things. We don't necessarily read things, but we see things. As in a classic high hurdle race, I put words in the art for people to jump a little higher. It seems silly to have a race where runners must hurdle over things, but that is the art of the race. Putting words into images is the art of the work as well; it presents multiple views that are on other levels.

A lot more information, just straightforward information, exists in our world today. We wear information on our chests now. Everybody has a shirt that says something about what he stands for or believes in. That's terrific. I write slogans that are not philosophy and not poetry. What I write does not come out of art. It may become art, but it comes from newspapers and magazines. It comes straight from culture.

I try to make my work frontal, straight; I try to avoid what I think might look arty. Because I do this, sometimes my art doesn't look serious. But I would hate for my art to be just for the art world. I don't see that that's so important a world. The art world has too narrow a definition; it's not big enough. I believe if you have something to say, it has to be accessible. You can't hide behind facades or aesthetic elitisms or any kind of posturing. I suppose I posture too, but when I do I'm obvious; that allows me to concentrate on the nature of the posturing.

Robert Arneson, 1983

George Segal

I started out as a painter years ago and became dissatisfied with the rules and limitations that my instructors placed on painting. I had a checkered school career. I bounced around at different places and finally transferred to New York University because abstract expressionists were teaching there. I was attracted to that kind of painting; I loved it. But it was a great surprise when I was given all those recipes: "Jump on the bandwagon of the history of art with us. Throw those small brushes away, get a big brush, get dried canvas, wipe your head out, put yourself in a trance, don't paint anything that you can see or touch." It was a baffling set of rules. What continued to attract me to the abstract expressionists over the years was their sense of morality, high purpose, and disembodied religion. They were antimaterialist; one was supposed to sneer at ordinary wealth. The painter's studio was a monastic cell devoted to the highest possible ideal. What made me rebellious was the necessity for shutting out what I could see with my eyes, shutting out the real world that I could see and touch. It wasn't until I switched to sculpture that I breathed much easier.

George Segal, 1981

Bryan Hunt, 1984

Bryan Hunt

I worry about running out of ideas all the time. Usually I come through with my best ideas on the threshold of "I have no ideas." I'm always on that step, on that threshold. It's a bit scary, but the more mature you are as an artist, the more you can understand yourself and the more you know you will catch yourself on the next step. Deep down you know that you will come up with new ideas and not lose it. You know it's there; you know your questions are there, your major doubts are there. I doubt myself more than most people doubt me. When I'm staring at a blank piece of paper, total doubt comes. And then the confidence comes, the momentum comes, and I suddenly find myself in the creative act.

John Baldessari

I tend to work in spurts; I sometimes might not work for three or four months. I just finished a period of working for about ten months for several exhibits. Now I'll go into hibernation for a while and think about what I've done, and I'll see whether the new work will be stillborn or enjoy a good life. I think about what ideas hold up for me, which ones don't, how an idea can be extended, or whether I've reached a dead end with it. This time is all evaluation and development. There are new works that I didn't exhibit, and I've got to determine why I thought they were unsuitable for showing. Quite often, I can't figure out something about them. Given more time, I might be able to.

I don't miss working while in this hibernation period. Other elements of life creep in. I've got stacks of books I haven't read yet, piles of letters to answer, phone calls I haven't returned. I've made several promises to do prints, I have a commission from a museum to finish, and a book I've been working on for three years that has to be completed. I feel, though, that I've got to spend some time ingesting. I can't always be putting out.

John Baldessari, 1984

Larry Rivers, 1982

Larry Rivers

Why do I still continue to have a lot of resistance? I think you have to be very old to be revered. You are criticized for a long time and then suddenly it all switches. It seems if you can outlive everybody, people want to be nice, finally. For example, Louise Nevelson is old enough now for everybody to say, "You're great, you're great."

But I still get lots of resistance. Not everyone thinks I'm a good artist. I'm known—everybody knows me— but it's different. Like Andy Warhol, I have a very strange career. Every show Warhol has, every single thing he does, is put down. It doesn't seem to stop anything; he's swinging. He's doing this, he's doing that, he's making $28 million a year. Every so often there's a person at a museum who doesn't listen to any of the criticism and gives Andy a show; so who the heck knows. Maybe it's the same thing with me. I think I have a different reputation from Andy. I don't seem as dependent on a certain part of society for my sustenance. Andy, in a way, is the favorite artist of those rich people who are really uninterested in art and more interested in themselves. And I get that too; it's a little depressing. A lot of people like my work; they don't buy the work, but they want a portrait of themselves done by me, which I'm finding very offensive, finally, as I get older. Why can't they just enjoy a painting of mine that has nothing to do with them?

Raymond Saunders

There are elements of and references to my child-hood in my work. For a long time I found it very difficult to relate to this because, as a black person, I felt that people would perceive me as naive, when in fact I know I am not. I want to be very skilled and present the skill in a credible fashion rather than hear, "He is a primitive," or "he is the child." That's ridiculous. Because of the history of blacks and whites, the history of what is America, one has to be careful when other people project who one is in a public forum. People have their vested interests, and for years interest in the black person was as someone who was naive, or primitive and spontaneous, rather than anything Western, cerebral, linear. I've had too much schooling to think of myself as either naive or childish, and yet I have an appreciation of those things that pertain to a very important time of my life. I mean, children paint beautifully, but as long as the designation "children's art" exists, there will be an undermining of their content. In some instances I seek the content of children's brilliance, which is no more or no less than the brilliance of any other time in life.

Raymond Saunders, 1982

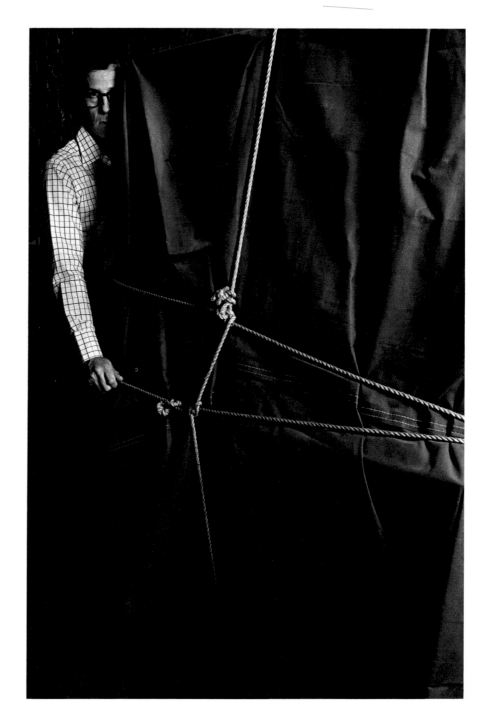

Christo, 1982

Christo

My projects are works of art with all the problems of creating artworks; there is no other justification to do them. They are never commissioned but are always initiated by me. I finance everything, and I am not obligated to nor do I owe anyone anything. These projects are the high joy of freedom. *Valley Curtain* was up for only twenty-eight hours, but still the engineers did it in the way I wanted it done. And to have it that way was great, even for twenty-eight hours, because I like to see these marvelous, crazy, visual things, which is illogical in any normal sense, but I don't care about that. I'm not involved with doing things that have some rational basis.

That my projects last only a few weeks is irrelevant. The short duration of the work of course puts many people off, causes a lot of discomfort. From the beginning, the projects are temporary because we only have a limited time to use the property. Technically they could stay longer, but they would require millions of dollars in maintenance—it's really like tending the gardens at Versailles, and I'm not into groundskeeping. I'm involved in the creative process, and I think that once the work is realized, the creative process is finished. I imagine that if the work lasted more than a few weeks it would look boring and might be annoying. I like the idea that a project will be gone, like a flower.

The fabric I use gives an essentially fleeting, ephemeral experience that causes a much more acute and nervous perception of the object by the public because tomorrow it may disappear. The wind, the forces, anything can damage it. The physical movement of the surface of the material creates great sympathy the way only something very fragile can arouse feelings. All that sympathy is extremely translatable to the people, and I find that very inspiring, very reflective of life. You cannot experience that with a sturdy material.

Dan Flavin, 1985

Dan Flavin

Years ago, when asked why I started arts of artificial light, I could not remember well enough to reply. I have supposed usually that I had assumed typical units of standard incandescent and fluorescent lighting as objects to be applied in profile to the perimeters of simple, square-fronted, one-colored, box-like constructions which could be installed anyplace—walls, floors, ceilings or, outside of architecture altogether. I presumed that, most importantly, I had intended a comparative interplay between the reflected return of so-called "paint light" and a lamp's projected illumination.

I named those lighted "paint things" icons, probably because of their apparent similarity to possible Russian religious ancestors and from a need to justify further their artistic existences through an added, respectable, art historical identification.

You know, the artistic comparison was not as interesting as that of art light alone; therefore, I decided to concentrate on that, thereafter.

I have already put lots of beautiful art of the artifice of artificial light into this world. By now, I prefer to be prompted on with it situationally. Offer me a site to light, and I will think about a relieving installation for it—the bigger, the better. (I sense typically American that way.)

A hard part is to provide distinct, comprehensive, and comprehensible art and utility simultaneously. And I have been practicing that practical problem for quite a while.

Well then, what's next? I don't know, but I do know that I am ready to respond.

© 1985 Dan Flavin

John Cage, 1984

John Cage

There is no room for emotion in a work of art. Rather, the emotion should be in the people who view the art. It's not good, in my opinion, when an artist puts emotion into his work and forces it on the observer. I don't like to be pushed around emotionally. I want to have my own emotions from my own, as we say, heart; I don't want to be forced to have the emotions that somebody else has.

Emotions are very little understood, even by psychologists. Being happy, for instance, is not really an emotion. The emotions were listed in ancient Indian philosophy as the heroic, the merciful, the erotic, and the wondrous—these were the white ones. The black ones were fear, anger, sorrow, and disgust. And the emotion that one should move toward was tranquillity, which had no color and was in the middle. If something makes you inordinately happy, it's to be questioned immediately. The same applies if something makes you sad. It should all move toward the middle. The movement in modern art now, neo-expressionism, is very emotional work. I can't respond to it; I don't find it interesting.

I don't try to be inspired; I just try to work very regularly. I don't work according to a schedule, but I'm always busy. I don't believe many artists are inspired. I think people who are not artists often feel that artists are inspired; but if you work at your art you don't have time to be inspired. I think most artists feel that being inspired is a myth. Simply put, out of the work comes the work.

There's a great deal of tedium in making almost anything. For instance, some of my recent etchings have 3,375 drawings around stones in them. That took me almost two months to make and it was tedious. While doing it, I began to think of the nature of what I was doing and what the nature of something different from that might be. This process leads me to the next work.

Keith Sonnier

Art making is a constant learning process. That's what makes it so interesting. It's a self-motivated investigation. I am an artist because I like that particular dynamic. I learn things about the world; I enhance my sense responses. I learn how things look, how things taste, how things smell because I employ those sense responses on a much broader level than I might in some other profession. I incorporate them in my work, so I'm sensitized to them. I tend to think the work that I make is about acculturation: I want to synthesize and alter culture.

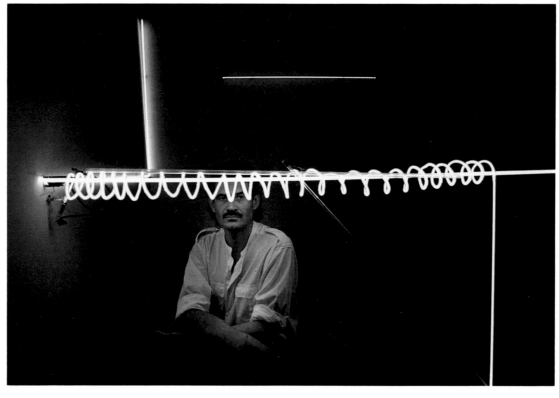

Keith Sonnier, 1983

Nam June Paik

It bothers me that video is not looked upon as a major art. I think art-world people look down on video. And television people look down on the art world as if we were all freaks. As a composer, I know that serious composers always look down on artists; they think anybody can paint. And painters and sculptors look down on video artists because they think anyone can easily do video, that one can just aim and shoot the camera. And we all look down on politicians, but really, politicians look down on us. So I guess everything is equal and goes round and round. And maybe photographers are at the bottom of the list; we'll see.

Nam June Paik, 1982

Susan Rothenberg

I start a canvas by gessoing it and making some marks on it, some marks of paint in black and white. I usually have a sense of what I want to do from my previous painting. Either I do nothing that I did in the last painting or I take it one step further. Sometimes I'll make a plan for a painting on the back of an envelope or on a slip of paper. I'll paint this here, this there, that here, to try it. I might just look at the preliminary sketch and rough it onto the canvas, and the painting is started. Then I apply more paint, scrape some off, more paint, paint it out, paint it black, paint it white, paint it black, paint it white again, paint it black again, and I'm under way. I sit in front of it and think about it between all the painting, and then it starts clarifying itself to me. It's all a struggle. If it weren't I'd be doing four paintings a day. It's just not simple; I don't know what should be there until it gets there.

Susan Rothenberg, 1982

Mary Beth Edelson, 1985

Mary Beth Edelson

I would like to sell more work to have more money so that I could do more with that money both politically and artistically. Money helps in every way; it helps to free up time, it helps to buy needed materials, and it helps to do some of the political things I want to do, to give to certain causes. Money is wonderful. It's ridiculous to think that artists don't need money as other people do. It's not true that if you don't have money you suffer more and therefore do better art. If you suffer more, you do worse art. The Van Gogh, cut-off-your-ear syndrome is just a worn-out notion people have. It's a stereotype of artists that has nothing to do with the realities of being an artist. Artists are very much like other people in relationship to needs, and the more they have to function with, the better they can function.

I'm looking forward to being rich and famous. Of course. Have you ever met an artist who doesn't want to be famous? Artists are the greatest delayed-gratification people in the world. It takes a very long time to build a career; we put up with so much for so many years. During that time we usually have to make do with very little; so there's got to be a pot of gold at the end of the rainbow. It isn't just a matter of money; there are lots of other pots of gold, such as recognition, which is what fame is. Recognition means that what you've done is worth something. If there is no recognition, there is no power, and I'm very interested in achieving enough power to get my ideas out. I loathe the idea of being powerless, which is something many women and minority groups have dealt with for a very long time. I'm committed not only to getting myself away from that, but also to pulling as many other people along with me as I can.

Louisa Chase

I don't know where the image of the cave came from in my paintings. I knew that I wanted to do an opening on the surface of the canvas that was very physical, such that one could enter into it. One could either be inside the cave looking out or outside the cave looking in. I think at one point when I started showing my work, I really wanted to hide out and the cave was a kind of retreat. I sort of wanted to hide from the outside world because there were a lot of demands being made, and I just wanted to go inside; I felt like I was being externalized too much. The demands were flattering, but at some point I just wanted to go back to those experiences I had when painting that really had nothing to do with the art world.

I don't think I'll be painting many more caves. That image is done; it's gone. I've left the cave now.

Louisa Chase, 1984

Michael Heizer

I made art all the time as a child and I simply continue to; I have never stopped. At home, I was allowed to make art if I wanted, but I wouldn't say I was encouraged any more than any other child. All children like to make art but are usually discouraged from doing it at a certain point, and they become inhibited about it. Maybe that just never happened to me. I did art on my own and not as a school-related activity. When adults talk to children about their art, children get confused and don't feel much like doing it anymore. People who survive the inhibitions and the self-consciousness of making art continue with it. There were no obstructions in my path to making art, so I'm an artist.

Michael Heizer, 1983

Michael Steiner

I just need to make art. My interest in the process of making art is something I can't really describe or place, but somehow I feel I'm doing what I need to do; it's no more complicated than that. If most people don't do what they need—say are in jobs that they hate—then maybe they don't need to do it enough. Maybe I'm doing art because my need for it is so great that whatever was necessary to arrive at doing it was something I was willing to experience or to chance.

There's no doubt in my mind that I will always make art. I do it the way I live my life, so I can't imagine being and feeling alive and not doing it. And when I say alive, I don't mean that if I am dead I can't do it. I'm talking about having the feeling of life in me. I feel that the art is coming from somewhere inside me where life is. As long as I feel alive, I will do art.

Michael Steiner, 1982

David Hare

I don't think young artists have more ideas than older artists; they just don't know the trouble they can get into, and they have enough energy to work day and night, to do a hundred different things. As I get older, I think my work is better, but I don't have the energy to do all those things that I'm not sure will turn out, and that's too bad. I have less physical energy than I did when I was thirty or forty years old, but I am more adept at what I'm doing; so it takes less energy to do it. It's not only a question of physical energy, though. I don't have the blind willingness to try something that might take six months to do and might be a total failure. I think, "Well, I won't do that; I'll do the other thing that is more likely to work." There are two points of view toward this attitude: you could say I am growing up a little and not wasting time, or you could maintain that I'm losing inventiveness because I'm not taking chances. Both are true. My work is better now, I think, than fifteen years ago, but back then I'd make a lot more mistakes, and every so often I'd get something that I could work from and continue on with. It might have been a mistake to begin with, but finally turned into something very interesting.

David Hare, 1982

Isabel Bishop

I've been an artist all my life, but recently I've not been that happy about being an artist because it's been frustrating. I think it's probably because I'm really getting old and it worries me. It's not harder physically for me to paint, but it's harder to bring things into a coherent form. I'm seventy-nine. I am old but I'm not used to it. Being old depends on how you age, and I'm worried about how I'm aging. I sort of counted on entering into a new phase of expression and it being a positive thing in my work, but I don't believe it for myself any longer.

People age differently, just physically age differently. Some people lose their hearing. I haven't lost that, but I think I've lost more important attributes. I don't see well; I had two cataract operations and now I have contact lenses. I think that's probably affecting my work because I can't count on what I see as being there. If I make deviations from what's there, that's OK, but I want to know what I'm deviating from.

I don't drink or smoke or go dancing too much. I try to take care of myself.

Isabel Bishop, 1981

Richard Artschwager

Painting and sculpture can be defined in terms of what the viewer does: a sculpture is something you look at and walk around, whereas a painting is something that you stand still to look at. There are certain definitions within mediums, but you can violate them once you've created your own territory. So let's reverse things. Let's have painting that's grabbable; sculpture that's not grabbable; sculpture that's uniform to the touch and feels the same anywhere it's touched, so that touching becomes a matter of indifference. Let's have painting that's bumpy and loaded with finger contact invitations, that can be walked around. Break the rules. The rewriting of the definitions of art in terms of what happens to the viewer is ever so interesting. My intent is always to make a stronger, more intense piece of art.

Richard Artschwager, 1984

Benny Andrews

I work a lot but I destroy much of it. I really don't need any new work. This is a funny thing to say because I exhibit a lot. But since I don't need more new work and I've always tried to work for myself, I don't really have to end up with anything. I don't have to go into the studio and paint another picture. There are too many already. My challenge is to produce a better piece of work, and it's a continuous struggle to do this. Every time I see an artist's retrospective, I come home and destroy more of my work. Most artists keep too much of their bad work. Ultimately, artists do very little good work. It's all in relation to yourself and what you believe.

Benny Andrews, 1982

Rhonda Zwillinger

Making art is the closest I get to God. It's when I either feel the most tortured with myself or the most at peace with myself. I've known that I would be an artist from the time I was first cognizant that I was a human being. I think the first instance I knew was when I was two-and-a-half or three years old. I was very bored, so one day my mother gave me a roll of toilet paper and a pencil and I started making sketches for a movie. From then on I knew I would be an artist, and it's always been my identity.

I'm really obsessed with making art. There's no separation between my life and my art, which is the way I like it. I'm supporting myself with my art and I don't want to be taken away from it; I just want to wrap myself, surround myself with it, so I can do the best work I can possibly do. I have so many ideas that I don't sleep at night. I don't go out a lot. I make art all the time; it's all I think about. It's almost as if I'm married to my art. It's almost like my jealous lover. It doesn't let me do anything else. Making art is part of my soul.

Rhonda Zwillinger, 1984

James Rosenquist, 1981

James Rosenquist

I have a list of thirty people waiting for my paintings. When such a list first starts to grow, I go to my shelf and pick out a tube of paint and mix it up to apply to the canvas. And I say, "When is this paint sold? Is it sold as I walk across the floor, is it sold when it touches the canvas, is it sold in my mind?" I once kidded around with a collector and said, "Would you like to buy this painting?" and showed him a blank canvas. I said, "I'm going to do this and that." And he said, "Well, uh, uh, I really can't buy it unless I can see it." He thought that I was seriously trying to sell him an empty canvas. I'll put it in a nutshell: when you start out, you work hard and if you are lucky, you sell paintings. As you grow older and older, someone comes along and says, "You know, now that you are successful we have to prepare for your death." You yell, "What do you mean prepare for my death? I haven't started yet; I'm still trying to make it."

You're really painting to make the best painting you can. A painting is like a companion—you make it, look at it, keep it, and then someone takes it away from you for money. Andy Warhol said something like, "Art is the art of making money." That may be for him, but I'm very self-conscious about trying to do the best I can to illuminate things for myself. You realize as time goes by that in spite of people offering you tons of money, you still won't let them have the painting unless it's a zinger.

I know a painting is finished when it looks all greasy and shiny and I'm happy.

Red Grooms

Having a professional art career is so different from what I originally envisioned it to be. It's so complicated because the career itself becomes something almost on its own. Originally you just make things. Eventually you've made enough art, and it's out there and people react to it whether you do or not. At this point half my time is spent with my career, just kind of curating and monitoring it, and the rest of the time I try to be as I used to be; I try just to do some art that's off the top of my head. I don't do as much art as I did in the past because I have a responsibility to look after the stuff. There's a kind of demand, too, from the outside, that is quite constant—the artist also is a personality. Many times I will be asked to give lectures or make a visit to an art school or an art-affiliated place. All of this monitoring and lecturing really doesn't have anything to do with my making art at all.

I like personalities; I've enjoyed other personalities very much. I like the magic and illusion involved in a personality, but at the same time it's a burden in that people will react to something they imagine, the illusion of who you are, when in fact you are just living a pretty mundane life simultaneously with the career. Still I perpetuate the illusion: part of it is actually my real personality and part I sort of fabricate out of the idea of making a personality. Sometimes I have to do this because there is a great deal of competition. I get tired of my career, but when I see it flagging I'm back out there fighting for my own territory and attention. A dealer of mine used to say that if you don't show every two years you will be forgotten—basically, it's true.

Red Grooms, 1982

Tom Wesselmann

I've been attacked a bit by feminists. They don't appreciate my work at all. At first I was offended that they should take that tack. I take the position—for example, in my bedroom paintings of women's breasts—of basic, innocent involvement. I may be making love to a woman and look up and see this beautiful breast. I become aware of what's around it—flowers, pillows, or whatever. And that's all it is to me. Women's lib has suggested that my work is a depersonalization of a woman that simplifies her down to a tit. It's a question of how you define art; that is, does art have to serve some sort of external philosophy. Well, it's an aspect of my life. I look up and I see this beautiful tit and I say "Wow, look at this beautiful tit," and I want to paint it. It's very exciting.

My goal is not to paint women. I don't feel obligated to paint all the social aspects of women, or the fact that women can succeed in business or can be smart or whatever. Women are wonderful creatures in all respects. When it comes to art, though, I'm interested in women visually, physically, basically sexually. But that doesn't mean that's all there is to women. I paint women's faces too. Of course, the problem with these faces is that an implied pleasure is taking place. Something is happening to her; she's digging it tremendously, like having sex or whatever. I mean, I don't spell it out. These paintings do represent also, in a sense, a certain degree of unfulfilled fantasy on my part—not a comment on women, not even a comment on how I feel about women, but certainly some sort of sexual wish on my part.

Tom Wesselmann, 1981

Duane Hanson

I sculpt a lot of big people—fat people. I just like their look; they have a presence about them that gives a certain weight to my work. To me, these people become beautiful. When I see a big person, I just stop and look because he or she strikes me as sculptural. I was looking for a real cleaning lady for this piece. I looked at five or six black ladies. Some weren't big enough; one was too old and couldn't stand up; one was too young. I always have in mind what I want to do, but if I don't have the right model, I'm not going to do the piece. I have this picture in my mind, and it must work all together to achieve an impact sculpturally. This particular big woman has worked hard and is going to be full of all kinds of clutter and mess. At first sight there is a certain amount of ugliness and dis-tastefulness connected with dirty mops and slop pails and all that stuff, but then there is, to me, a truthfulness about one who works so hard, about the very basic struggling of the lower-middle-class working people who just get along doing drudgery. In a lot of lives a lot of drudgery has to be done. I have no objections to sculpting a beautiful woman, but I feel that I can do more with this kind of subject. There is a certain tragic quality that enters into my work, a dramatic quality that I like.

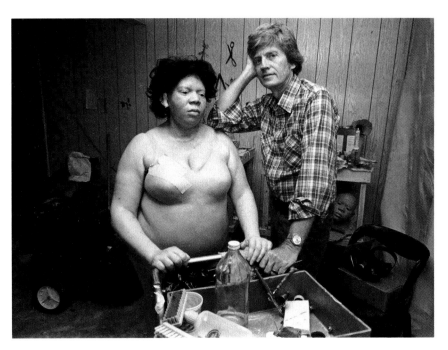

Duane Hanson, 1980

Mary Frank

I'm not interested in going down in history. That doesn't have a lot of meaning for me. If something is written that is really insightful about my work, good, but posterity has very little value for me. I think fame is a terrible reason to do art. For me, the reason to do art is that it's compelling. Art is a drive, a very complex desire and need, urgency and pleasure. I think the need shows in my work. The work is quite available; it's not very esoteric, and so those needs are there. For that reason I don't feel it's necessary to talk much about it.

I feel that working is being part of a continuum from a distant past; people have always had to invent forms of all kinds to deal with their primary needs and desires of what it is to be human on this earth.

Mary Frank, 1981

David Salle

I have to quote that often-quoted line by Barnett Newman: "An artist paints so that he will have something to look at." It's the hyperbole of hyperboles, but it's perfectly true. There's no other reason to make art. You just make it because you want to see it, and no one else is going to make it. It's not a question of wanting to see just anything. If someone else could make the art that evokes the same kind of experience when looking at it that my art does, then I probably wouldn't have to do it.

David Salle, 1982

Richard Hambleton

It's upsetting to get a bad review. In some cases the critic is writing an opinion based not on the work, but on something else, and that can be especially upsetting. I don't think bad reviews can break an artist or stop him from making art. But the artist's career won't be helped by a bad review, whereas a good review can probably help sell his work. Critics have the power to make somebody important. But when critics aim to harm an artist—and I know a few of them do—it can be damaging to the artist, but not to the work. The work will continue. Sometimes it's better for the artist not to say too much, to play dumb. Let the critics do it all.

Richard Hambleton, 1983

Leon Polk Smith

As soon as I finished school, the first thing I did was to break all the rules that my instructors told me to follow. I started basing most of my work on their *don'ts*, which appealed to me more than the things they said to do. It seemed that everybody was doing the *dos* and so much of it was bad. I found a challenge in the *don'ts*. It wasn't a matter of rebelling. I remember a teacher saying a *don't* was that at the corner of a canvas there already were two lines converging at a point; so you shouldn't start in the corner of a canvas with a third line because that would complicate everything. This fascinated me; this, I wanted to do and I did. The work was successful, strong, and unique. One *do* was to use heavy color at the bottom of the painting because gravity pulls heavier things down. But I was not painting gravity, especially after I started to paint abstractly. That instruction had nothing to do with what I worked on. I'm not painting gravity; I'm not painting earth. So I wanted to have all my heavier colors—bright reds, blacks—at the top and lighter colors at the bottom. It produced paintings that were different from what people were used to seeing.

Leon Polk Smith, 1982

Donald Judd, 1982

Donald Judd

Talent is a rather arbitrary word. It's virtually a cliché. I'm not too sure what people mean when they say talent. There has to be some natural interest and ability for an artist to work with. Beyond that, I think it takes intelligence and wit, a lot of both, to be an artist. Many people presumably have talent, but if they don't do anything with it, it doesn't matter how much talent they have. I don't know whether talent is God-given, but it's given, I think. You may develop it or you may not, depending on the circumstances. I think if it's not given, you can't do anything about it. You do something else besides art.

I think the broad populace is not interested in art, and I don't necessarily expect them to be. Too much is being asked of art to expect millions of people to be interested in it. Art is not a sport; it's not the superbowl. Great popularity is not going to happen. And although Mary Boone is put on the cover of *New York* Magazine, it's nothing compared to Burt Reynolds's popularity.

I don't think being famous is a necessity for artists. They are not famous the way movie stars or politicians are famous; they're not known by the general public. I don't think that's a particular problem. I consider doing art a rather special activity, and either people are interested in it or they are not. I'm not perturbed by those who are not interested; I'm perturbed by those who just play with it. They are the ones who are causing the trouble.

Andy Warhol

If you want to know all about Andy Warhol, just look at the surface of my paintings and films and me, and there I am. There's nothing behind it.

Exhibition catalogue, *Andy Warhol*
Moderna Museet, Stockholm, Sweden, 1968

Interviewer: What is Art?
Andy Warhol: It's . . . a boy's name.

The Hamptons Newspaper/Magazine
July 23, 1981, p. 18

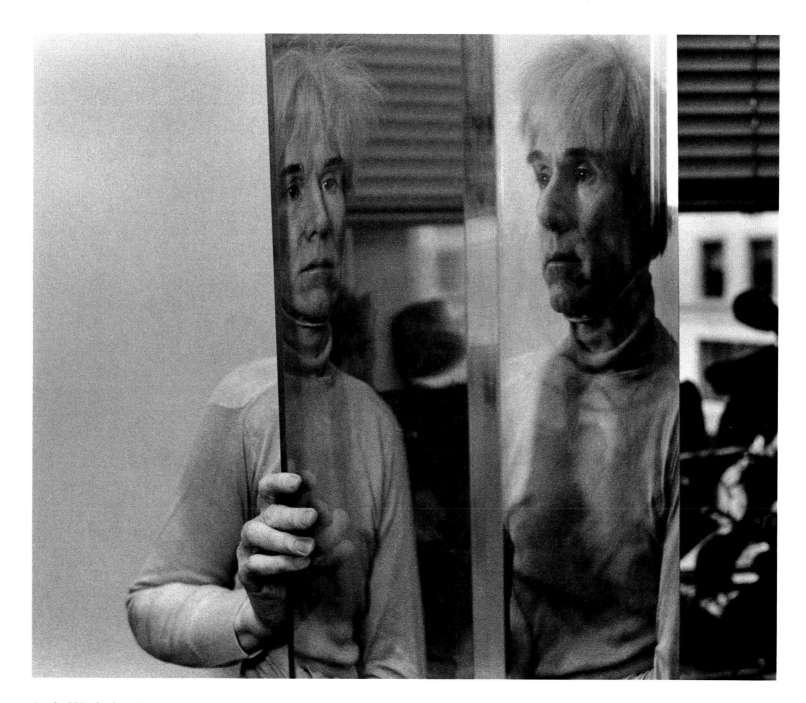

Andy Warhol, 1983

Lee Krasner

I was always outraged by the bias that I experienced as a woman artist. The bias was not up front where you could get ahold of it. It was behind the back. The bias was just washed over; people would say, "It's your imagination, it's in your mind."

The other prejudice against me occurred after I married Jackson Pollock and became attached to his name, both as a wife and as a widow. That was the final washout. Believe me, it was a heavy load. I have always gone by the name Lee Krasner as a painter. I never used the name Pollock in connection with my work. I am Mrs. Pollock, but I've been Lee Krasner, I am Lee Krasner, and that name was used right through the marriage as well. The fact that people didn't know or didn't acknowledge it was their hang-up. Whenever people called me Lee Pollock concerning work, I had a fit. I don't want Lee Krasner Pollock; I don't want the name Pollock as an artist. I am Lee Krasner. I'm called Pollock when I can't control it or when I've nothing to say about it. Nor can I say I'm not Mrs. Pollock; I can't deny that, and that's one of the things I deal with. I just fully expect to be called Lee Krasner and not Lee Krasner Pollock.

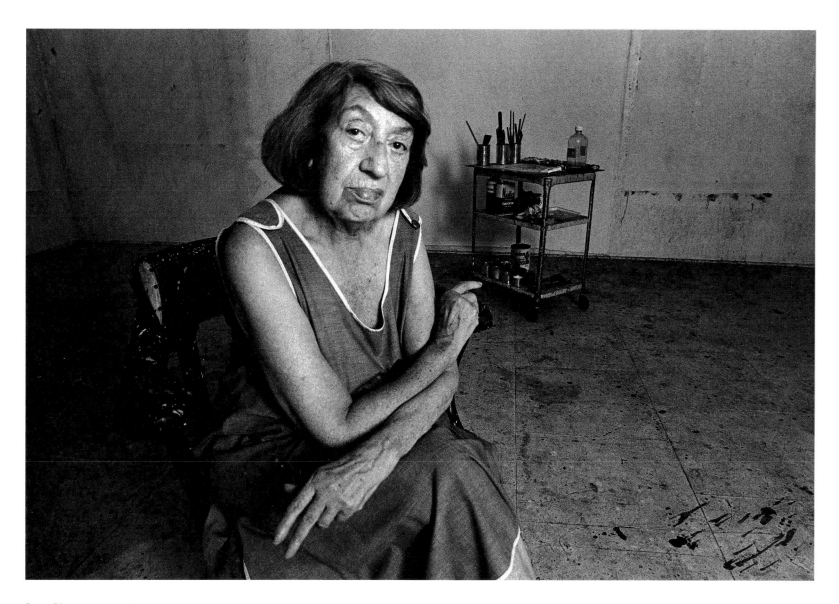

Lee Krasner, 1982

Jennifer Bartlett

I don't know whether or not artists have strong egos, but they seem to. I'm appalled by mine. It's certainly not too small; it errs on the too-big side. It seems riveting to me when I say I like chocolate cake, but I do have enough awareness to realize that occasionally this might be less than interesting to other people. A classic Freudian definition of a weak ego would be someone who needs to incorporate the world and see it totally from his or her own point of view. This sounds like what artists do, but I don't know if that is weak or strong. Most artists I know seem to have strong opinions about particular ways of living, various likes and dislikes, and that falls roughly into the area of being concerned with oneself, whether negatively or positively. But most artists I know think their work is terrible; they are perpetually self-doubting and are extremely anxious. I've heard very few artists whom I know well say, "You've got to come and see this piece; it's great." I usually hear, "This piece is horrible; it's a disaster. Come and tell me what to do with it."

Jennifer Bartlett, 1982

Julian Schnabel

Art is the medium between me and the world.

It fits me into the world.

The physical fact of a painting is for the painter (or let's say for me) a microcosm of the world. And I hope it can be a handbook for others.

I don't like to think that my paintings only refer back to myself. Through a quality of seeing one can have the recognition of shared humanness and thought, and of course I mean feelings.

Art gets made out of the need for some direct, concrete truth that stays intact for as long as the work exists.

It's just a way to cheat death.

Julian Schnabel, 1983

Valerie Jaudon

I learn a tremendous amount from having exhibitions. After I finish hanging a show, I usually walk out and come back in and see the work in a fresh way, really for the first time. In those ten or fifteen minutes, I discover what is wrong with everything in the show. It's so clear to me, so apparent, at those moments. It's a very special time, and I always know it's coming. It shocked me the first time it happened, but now I look for it; it's some of my favorite time. If anyone is with me, there's no way to tell that person anything. That time is strictly between the work and me. And I'm almost planning my next show, telling myself what is wrong with this one. I just see the work with a real clarity that I couldn't when all of it was in the studio, lined up and finished. Somehow being exposed to the public crystallizes everything. It's not so much that I'm seeing flaws in the work. When I have a show I'm putting the very best I can do at the moment out there. But what I'm doing is learning for the next painting. I would really dread it if I looked at a show and said, "My God, it's perfect." Then I could never do anything else.

Valerie Jaudon, 1982

Jack Levine

Some people decree that narrative painting, with its hundreds of years of magnificent history, shouldn't happen any longer. But why not do it? It's fraught with thrilling possibilities. Who the hell, as they say, died and left them boss? They can't even draw a foot, and they are handing down edicts about what art should be. Nobody has any right to hand out edicts in this business. These people are supposed to take what the artist does as given and do the best they can with it. They are never supposed to suggest that it would be better if the artist did this and not that. By these people, I mean writers on the subject of art who try to mold artists and are partisan—it's a little bit like having a dictated psychoanalysis. Art is not supposed to happen that way. I remember when John Canaday, a former *New York Times* art critic, said that there ought to be a moratorium on painting. He was wrong. There ought to be a moratorium on writing about painting; that's where the trouble is. Then maybe artists could find themselves. If all those bystanders and meddlers would bug off, the artist might find out what he wants to do.

Jack Levine, 1981

Pat Olezsko

When I go out wearing a costume, I create this incredible traveling circus of people who follow me. I can be arrested and hauled off by the police, whatever. I create these funny, funny situations that seem to happen constantly; my life becomes a series of crazy anecdotes. New York is filled with hundreds of opportunities to do this, but the situations also exist by themselves. Every day something totally outrageous happens, and I'm just part of it.

Sometimes it's more necessary to create these happenings, although not in New York because these things happen here anyway. My life's ambition is to go to every college in Ohio because they need some life; everything is so dull, so plain there. For me, it's actually more important to do performances there and in North Dakota because people there will talk about it for thirty years. I have a great following there; they really like me. You can't believe it. I know what it's like; I grew up in the Midwest. I remember when a visiting artist came to my college; I remember when I was very young and I saw the circus. I thought, "How can life be like that? Can you live that way and always pay attention to the absurd?" I try to create my art with this in mind.

Pat Oleszko, 1981

Sandy Skoglund

When I was in graduate school, I did work that was somewhat similar to what I'm doing now, except it wasn't as fleshed out or as extensive. Then I came to New York when minimalism was in its heyday, and I became consumed, enthralled by it. My paintings consisted of dots just covering the canvas. Those paintings led me to a tremendous, horrible dead end, and it was reflected in my life. The distance, the boredom, every aspect of doing that kind of work was reflective of the way I was living. And it was very difficult to work myself out of it. One of the reasons that I'm doing my current work is because I'm reacting against minimalism, against work that places certain kinds of ideas first. The work itself exists in the flesh, and its presence and physicality are more important than the idea.

I don't think it's entirely appropriate for me to be called a photographer, but I'm not the only one it's happened to. There is a whole wave of photography being done by people with backgrounds not in photography. I think, though, that it's very interesting, fascinating, in fact, that the photography world is so open to looking at my work and accepting it as photography. I'm comfortable being called a photographer rather than a sculptor or painter, even though I have painted and sculpted for years. The label doesn't matter to me; it's not something that should matter. The work is what matters.

Sandy Skoglund, 1982

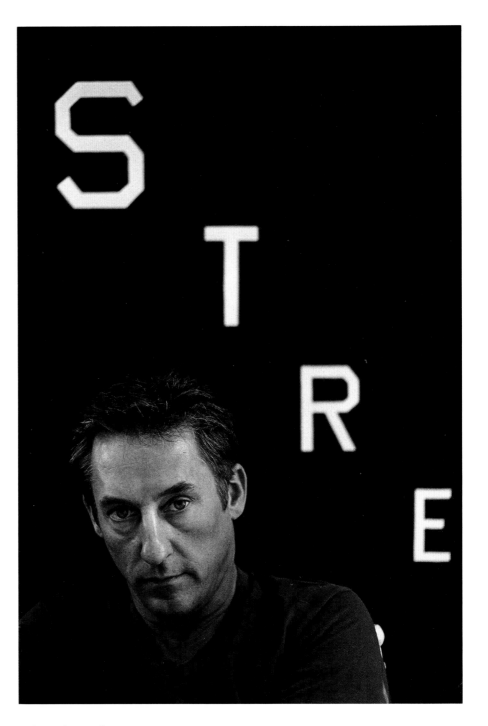

Edward Ruscha, 1984

Edward Ruscha

Careerwise, I'd be better off if I lived in New York City. An artist gets penalty points for living in California, as far as the art goes. It's more difficult to live away from a major center like New York, and that's why I tell all the younger artists to go there.

It's been slower here, but I've survived because I live in Los Angeles. My work would be in more shows if I lived in New York, but I might not be painting today. If I lived there, I think I would have been spit out; I would have ended up in a dumpster somewhere because it's such a fast world there. There's just something that makes me jittery about it. But when I go back to New York I like being there; yeah, I love it. It's a hot city. I just don't want to live there. New York seems a little crueler, harder; someone's always after you. You can't walk out on the street without something happening. It's not that way in Los Angeles; it's much easier to live here. I think perhaps there would be more anxiety in my work if I lived in New York. You don't know how those things come into play, but it's probably so. Your work is a part of how and where you live.

Keith Haring, 1982

Keith Haring

I'm always working and drawing; there's nothing else to do. It's just what I can do, so I do it. And that's one big advantage of being an artist instead of an actor or a writer or an athlete: I really don't have to depend on anybody. I don't even need a pencil; I can draw with my finger in dust, I can draw with a stick in the sand.

I thought my art was about people seeing it, and that meant getting it out through a lot of different channels. I didn't want to be an artist so that only people in galleries would see it. On the other hand, I didn't want my art only seen in the subway where it couldn't be part of the mass media of television or magazines. There are many other media in which a work of art can function and become part of the world. The work in the gallery reinforces the work in the street and only opens up more possibilities. Getting asked to do things on television immediately takes the art from an audience of hundreds or thousands to millions of people; who would turn that down?

Success doesn't necessarily have to be an evil thing. The only thing that makes it evil is the association with dollars and cents, and I don't think money is necessarily evil either. Look at the incomes of successful actors and actresses, baseball players, musicians; that's the way the world runs. There is no reason artists have to be outside that system. Once success happens, it doesn't mean that suddenly the art is not good or that you've sold out. You can also use success as a vehicle to do bigger things or to get the art to more people. But there is a danger. It's like walking a thin line; you put yourself in a very precarious situation because suddenly everybody is watching, everybody is trying to make you fall. As soon as you get any amount of attention for something, you receive equal amounts of attack. I never had enemies before my work started to sell.

Barbara Siegel

After a while you realize that being an artist is not as glamorous as people think. The fortune to be made, except for a very few artists, is nonexistent. There was a time when I thought that to have a painting in a museum exhibit would be the ultimate. Then it happened and it wasn't the ultimate. The next day I was back in my studio still trying to figure out what I was doing. Then I thought if a museum would buy a painting, that would be it. A museum bought a painting and I still had to pay the rent. I was back where I started. I'm a lot more realistic now; I get more and more realistic all the time.

The life I lead would probably be frightening to most traditionally oriented people. There's no one to measure me, to tell me what to do or to say I'm doing a good job. I don't get an automatic salary increase or any kind of guidance. There are no rituals to an artist's life, no clock to tell me when I must get up, go to work, or leave for home. It's not an external life; it's all internal. I'm totally on my own with no one to blame or congratulate but myself.

Barbara Siegel, 1982

Alice Neel

If I weren't an artist, I'd get so morbid and so bored, but this way my life is very lively. I travel all over the country and have shows everywhere. I can't go so far as to say that painting keeps me alive, but I think an interest in life keeps me alive. I think a lot of old people die because their lives are empty and they just sit in a chair with nothing to do. I never was that way; I never have time for all I want to do.

My work certainly has not always been accepted. For one thing, critics thought I was too rough on people. But that's ridiculous. You don't want those insipid things that pass for portraits. Who wants that? I told too much truth, and they didn't like it. It was definitely hard to sell my work. I always had shows, but I was not kosher. People don't want to be diagnosed. They do more so now because they are more intelligent. Although I painted all those years, I never got any real recognition until 1960 when I was published in *Artnews*; then in 1974 I had a big show at the Whitney Museum. From the late 1950s I began to get reviews and noticed a lot, but the reviews didn't mean anything. The fact is that they wanted some insipid little spot on the canvas during abstract expressionism's popularity. So definitely, I'd say that my recognition has come late to me. Anybody would be upset by that.

Alice Neel, 1980

Romare Bearden

I once read in Delacroix's journal that he copied paintings. Now people feel that's too pedantic to do, but I think that's the greatest way of learning how to paint. I took three years off from painting and got big sheets of brown paper and shellacked them. I started with Giotto and copied him and then Veronese right on down to the modern painters. I even did a Matisse. The only painting that I could not deal with at all was Rembrandt's *Pilate Washing His Hands* at the Metropolitan Museum. I found that Rembrandt was the most mysterious of painters; the relationships in his paintings are so vague, so hidden, and every time you look you see more.

So I did nothing else but copy paintings; that was my study of art and how to put a picture together. That was part of my education. Painting and art cannot be taught. You can save time if someone tells you to put blue and yellow together to make green, but the essence of painting is a self-disciplined activity that you have to learn by yourself.

There are no goals that I still want to reach. I don't believe in goals; goals are for a football team. An artist is just seeking what he might find.

Romare Bearden, 1982

Will Barnet

Sometimes I get an idea that's good right away, but it takes me a while to get the parts to fit. I leave sketches on my wall. I study them, I come back and make changes, eliminate, put in, take out, so that it's a matter of much deduction. For me, each painting takes several months. The months, like the aging of a good wine, give a certain richness to it.

I build up my paintings so that after a while I can tell whether a painting has the proper light. That light is very important to me in the relationship of warm to cool colors. I usually put the painting in a dark room to see if it has the right luminosity and whether I can see the forms I've painted. If I can, then I know it's alive, but if it stays dark in a dark room, then I know it's wrong. Then I have to go back to the canvas and repaint it until I feel the luminosity and feel the light coming through.

Will Barnet, 1980

Colette

I can't help wearing costumes; it's my personal style. I wear them outdoors because it's almost organic for me to do so. Costumes are like skin to me. They are a statement too: I don't think about anything I do but at the same time I think about everything I do. I try to make everything harmonize with itself. I'm creating environments; I live in my environment, I look like my environment, I carry part of the environment with me when I leave my studio. By going out in costume, I feel I am living my art and am connected to it all the time. Costumes are a means of dealing with modern times, but in a fantasy way that is in accord with my lifestyle. I live in a space that's total fantasy, yet it functions. It works as any space does, except that it looks like fantasy. The costumes are a practical way of resolving the idea of dressing and simultaneously being very visual and directly involved in my work. I've always felt I looked somewhat like my work.

Of course I want to be famous. I'm sure there are good and bad reasons for wanting fame. One side of me enjoys being public, and being famous is being public. There isn't any point in being an artist and trying to make a statement if no one knows that you're doing it. Being famous has to do with communication. If you do the best art in the world, but no one knows about it, or you can't communicate it or give it to someone, then it's all a waste. What I fear most is that my work will be destroyed and nobody will know about it.

Colette, 1981

Judy Pfaff

Most artists live with a lot of drudgery in their lives. It's certainly not a glamorous life. Most of the artists I know work really hard. Actually, most of the rich people I know work really hard. The glamour part is one percent. At my recent opening, I could hardly see straight. I hadn't slept for a long time in getting the show ready, and still it wasn't finished when it opened. But the opening was terrific. People were saying hello and I was high as a kite. I was very happy. But that was all a moment; it was like being on top of the world for one minute. That night also, I thought, "God, I'm tired, and I've got to get things out of the basement. I've got to move this over here...." I actually had to go to Buffalo and take a show down the day after my New York opening; so it was such a fleeting moment.

How do you know if the show will be well-received? You can't predict it; there's such anxiety. One year an artist is the king of the castle and the next year every review says his new show is a bomb. As glamorous as an artist's life may be, there's so much that isn't glamorous. Despite all this, being an artist is the only place where I can think clearly and learn what being alive is all about.

Judy Pfaff, 1983

Mark di Suvero

The art-world system inadvertently works to fix artists so that through success they are kept in the same slot that they're used to. One is encouraged to repeat, discouraged to explore and radically shift the nature of his terrain and viewpoint. Part of the responsibility of the artist is to follow and direct his work toward the maximum of experience. Sometimes this responsibility means abandoning what one can do well and what one knows, and going away from the success symbol, the salable item, or the commodity view in order to proceed in a direction that is unpopular. But the system—galleries, even museum people—tends to penalize people who do that. Someone might say, "That's not what you're known for"; "it's the wrong material"; or "it's shiny and it should be rusty"; or "it's bronze and we expected plaster." There's a real pressure that way.

Courage is one of the very essential things in any artist's exploration. You have to be able to go where they say it doesn't exist. Thoreau said something like, "The original vision is nothing but seeing as it is, not as they've told you it is." He did a lot for me.

Mark di Suvero, 1983

William Wegman, 1982

William Wegman

I miss my dog, Man Ray, who died last week, more as a pet than as an art partner. I knew his death was going to happen; I was very aware of it since 1977 when he almost died. I got five more years from him, so I am happy about that. I started to use him a lot in my work after his mortality became so immanent. In a way I felt I might be working myself into a corner. I'd use him about one of twenty times during the first seven years of his life but more so as he grew older, perhaps in a desperate urge to keep him alive.

He was conditioned from six weeks old to be in front of the camera; it became part of his daily activity. It's rather cute to say that he looked forward to working, but I'm not really sure of that; he didn't hate it at all. There were certain things that annoyed him—like being spray-painted—but he would put up with it. Video, especially, was part play, part work to him. It was some sort of engagement. There were some work things that he really liked, but whether he was fond of keeping still for half an hour for a photograph I don't know; maybe, maybe not. But he could do it well. He knew what a camera was, that was obvious. He knew what lights were, and that he was going to do certain things. Toward the end he was lame in his rear legs. He'd see the platform, walk over to it and put his front legs up on it, and just wait for me to hoist him up from the back. Then he'd face the camera and become limp. I'd climb up there to push him sideways or lay him down, and he knew he was working again.

Lucas Samaras, 1981

Lucas Samaras

I haven't been going down to Soho, but I like the idea of its existence. Even when Soho was just starting to happen, I thought it was wonderful. So I like it; I just end up not going there. Partly it has to do with ego; that is, if I'm here on the West Side, nobody knows me and it's fine. But if I'm in an art area, then I want my power as an artist to be exercised. If I'm walking on the street in Soho, I want people to stand at attention. It's unreasonable of me, but I can't help it. It's a very disturbing experience. This happens even if I go to a museum, whenever I'm in an area where art is being made or sold or promoted. If people don't respond to me in an artistic environment, I don't feel right, so I usually avoid going there. I avoid going to museums now. The only place where I don't feel that competitiveness is the Museum of Natural History, because there nature has done the work, not another artist.

I think whenever I feel comfortable or wanted, it's as if I've received a gift and can say, "Let me take a rest." This feeling is like finding a desert oasis for a very brief duration, because I know in a short time I will not feel safe; so I have to get as much oxygen as I can, as much nourishment for the next trek through the desert. I don't know why the feeling is so short-lived. That's my life; that's the pattern. That's how it's been, and I have made it work for me. Whenever I felt separated from everybody else I said, "Fuck it, I'm going to go to work," and I made art. I work all the time, regardless. I don't know how much of my work is produced under masochistic conditions. If I feel loved, it's as if I've become pregnant, and when I get into a period of rejection and feel that nobody loves me, then I produce the baby, the art. The birth takes place usually when no one is around, because then I have to produce it in order to survive.

Robert Rauschenberg

When I started out as an artist, I did not think I would be successful; I still don't think I am. I work for myself. The other thing is fickle; all this success could fall apart overnight. I don't think it would bother me if it did, but I'm not sure. For now, for my lifetime, it seems that I am considered a top artist and that doesn't surprise me. But this doesn't help me to make a new work. I go to work every time thinking, "What on earth am I going to do? How will I make something that works?" Everything else is just facts, figures, and opinions. Thank God that fame doesn't help me make the art. It would get in the way if I started to believe I was a good artist. Then I would have to make good art. I asked Bill de Kooning once, "How do you feel about people who paint all these great De Koonings?" He answered, "But they can't do the bad ones." So I have my own territory there; I can do the bad Rauschenbergs. I go to work every day hoping that I can do another bad Rauschenberg. And those are the good ones.

Robert Rauschenberg, 1985

For Sara, Louis, and Hilda
without whose love, patience, and understanding
this book (and my existence) would not be possible

HARVEY STEIN began as a professional photographer in 1972, and he has taught the subject since 1976. His photographs have been widely published—in *Time, Life, Newsweek, The New York Times, Artnews, Smithsonian, American Photographer*, and many other periodicals—and exhibited in the United States and Europe. His work is represented in numerous collections, including those of the Art Institute of Chicago, the Brooklyn Museum, the International Center of Photography, the Corcoran Gallery of Art, the American Museum of Natural History, and the Polaroid Collection. A recipient of the 1982/83 Creative Arts Public Service fellowship, Stein currently teaches at the International Center of Photography and the University of Bridgeport. His first book, *Parallels: A Look at Twins*, was published in 1978.

CORNELL CAPA, a former *Life* magazine photographer, is an author, editor, curator, and Founding Director of the International Center of Photography in New York.

ELAINE A. KING, an art historian who has organized numerous exhibitions of contemporary art, is currently Assistant Professor of Art History and Director of the Carnegie-Mellon University Art Gallery in Pittsburgh.

Project Director: Robert Morton
Editor: Harriet Whelchel
Designer: Michael Hentges

Library of Congress Cataloging-in-Publication Data

Stein, Harvey.
    Artists observed.

    Includes index.
    1. Artists—Interviews. 2. Artists—Psychology.
3. Artists—Portraits. I. King, Elaine A. II. Title.
NX165.S73   1986   700'.92'2   85–20144
ISBN 0–8109–2325–4 (pbk.)

Published in 1986 by Harry N. Abrams, Incorporated, New York.
All rights reserved. No part of the contents of this book may be reproduced without the written permission of the publishers.

Front cover: Larry Rivers   Printed and bound in Italy